UNBREAKABLE

*Heroic Stories of Triumph
Over Trauma*

COMPILED BY

JENNIFER NIELSON

UNBREAKABLE
Heroic Stories of Triumph
Over Trauma

Copyright © 2022 by Jennifer Nielson

To request permissions, contact the publisher at
contact@freedomhousepublishingco.com or jnielson92@gmail.com.
Paperback ISBN: 978-1-952566-78-3
eBook ISBN: 978-1-952566-79-0

Printed in the USA.
Freedom House Publishing Co
Middleton, ID 83644
www.freedomhousepublishingco.com

FREEDOM HOUSE
PUBLISHING CO

Disclaimer

All of these stories are the authors' own memories and personal truths. Where it has been applicable; names and locations may or may not be the original.

Neither Freedom House Publishing Co. nor Jennifer Nielson holds any liability for their portrayal of their personal circumstances.

The publisher and the author are providing this book and its contents on an "as is" basis and make no representations or warranties of any kind with respect to this book or its contents. In addition, the publisher and the authors assume no responsibility for errors, inaccuracies, omissions, or any other inconsistencies herein.

Although the author and publisher have made every effort to ensure that the information in this book was correct at press time, the author and publisher do not assume and hereby disclaim any liability to any party for any loss, damage, or disruption caused by errors or omissions, whether such errors or omissions result from negligence, accident, or any other cause.

The information, views and opinions contained and expressed in this content represents the views and opinions of the authors. It does not necessarily represent or reflect the opinions and beliefs of Freedom House Publishing Co. and Jennifer Nielson.

FIND YOUR STORY

Unbreakable is not a religiously affiliated book, the authors within this book share their own personal stories and accounts connected to their own personal religious backgrounds and affiliations.

Each chapter has a message for certain readers. If a chapter does not apply to you and your life, we invite you to move forward and find the stories that resonate with you.

This book is here to awaken your *Unbreakable* story.

TABLE OF CONTENTS

Unbreakable

INTRODUCTION

Pain is inevitable, part of our human experience. What sets us apart is not the pain. It's how we deal with it and who we become.

Most of us have faced some kind of trauma—financial struggles, betrayal, physical or sexual abuse, death, divorce, or a life-altering accident. Over the past few years, traumatizing events outside of our control have upended our lives on a global level.

And if we don't heal that trauma, it will destroy us from the inside out. Unresolved issues adversely affect our careers, our personal relationships, and even our health.

I know trauma and pain. Intimately. The "I'm not sure I can survive this" kind of pain.

I've gone to great lengths to heal my own pain and trauma.

When I think back to the worst of my suffering, I refer to that as the drowning stage. At the time, it was hard to imagine an existence without pain and suffering. Hope seemed out of reach. But with some help, I clawed my way out of the black hole and found some comfort in counseling and other resources.

Then I found myself in the treading water stage. I continued collecting tools and knowledge through various modalities, and my outlook improved incrementally, but something was missing. It was as if I relied on all these external resources to fill me up the way a car needs a gas station. But if you're a car in the middle of nowhere, without a gas station in sight, what do you do? I didn't want to rely on someone or something else to fix me. I knew I would not reach the thriving stage until I learned to do the most important thing: heal myself.

I wanted to be self-powered, independent, and unstoppable.

And I vowed that once I cracked the code on self-healing, I would help others do the same so they could go from drowning to treading water to thriving.

That is when The Dig was born—a groundbreaking, self-healing process that helps anyone who feels broken, hopeless, stuck, worthless, or powerless to start living a life filled with freedom, fulfillment, and joy.

It has been a privilege and honor to help women find this kind of freedom by implementing The Dig in their lives.

I've worked with countless women who are now dedicated to breaking free from their trauma so that they can grow into the best version of themselves. With The Dig in their toolbox, nothing can hold them back.

And in this book, you get to hear from 12 of those brave women.

In our noisy world full of digital distractions and people vying for our attention and admiration, these women are the true heroes. They are real women who have overcome the impossible and now inspire others to do the same.

While each story is unique, the experiences are relatable, and the common thread of resilience makes the collection inspirational. Their stories of abuse, divorce, betrayal, disease, and unexpected twists and turns will show you that no matter what you've been through, you too can thrive.

The power to overcome and conquer adversity is within all of us.

1

BEYOND THE FISH BOWL
By Tanya Burdick

PART 1: The Fish Bowl

Maya Angelou once said, "People will forget what you said, people will forget what you did, but people will never forget how you made them feel." I heard that quote after I was married. At the time, I didn't realize the impact that it would have on my whole existence.

I don't have a lot of memories of my growing up years. Mostly just negative ones. I was reading *It Didn't Start with You* by Mark Wolynn, and it explains this thought process. It is an extremely interesting book, and one part in particular resonated with me. Wolynn writes that, as small children, we experience both comforting and unsettling times, and often, the comforting memories seem to be blocked from surfacing. He says, "When we, as small children, experienced our safety or security being threatened, our bodies reacted by erecting defenses." In those moments, our attention is directed to what's difficult instead of comforting and the good memories stay on the other side of a wall, just out of reach. It's as if we are rewriting history as the defenses that have been with us for so long begin to become us. We worry that if we recall any loving, tender moments with our parents, we would feel vulnerable and risk being hurt again.

This seems to be a recurring theme for me. Not only with my parents (especially my mother), but with anyone that came too close.

For as long as I can remember, I've experienced feelings of fear, rejection, and being overlooked. I felt pushed aside, like an afterthought. I was always consumed with the perceptions of others. Have you ever felt like you don't belong? Not just a fleeting feeling, but the overwhelming anxiety that you really do not know where you fit in? That left-in-the-outskirts feeling has been my constant companion for as long as I can remember. Always nagging, always nipping at my heels. Never letting me forget my place—or lack thereof.

I am a visual person. Emotions form pictures in my head, and I have a couple of images that I'd like to share. The first is an outline of a body, but this is a vertical form. Negative emotions are stuffed into this form. It reminds me of trying to stuff a sleeping bag back into its cover after you've used it. They never fit the same. At some point, the emotions overflowed and burst from the top. That is when I would yell, scream, or lash out with words I could not take back— just spewing ugliness in my wake.

The next visual in my head is a fish tank. Some say that a fish's growth potential is determined by its environment (i.e., the tank size, water level, PH balance, food, etc.). I see myself as a fish. It doesn't matter what kind—just a fish in a small bowl. My environment was less than ideal growing up and I wasn't allowed to reach my potential. All the things I mentioned earlier were taking up space.

PART 2: My Mother

Like I mentioned earlier, I cannot pinpoint anything specific that was done to me—it was just a feeling of being an afterthought.

I can tell you that any emotions I did have were not enough. Fear, worry, and even hunger were considered lesser than my mother's feelings. If I was hungry, she would tell me that I don't know what hunger is because she had only a potato to share with her family and extended family. So, I should stop complaining because I don't know how good I have it.

My mother grew up during World War II. Her life was hard and she suffered and saw many unthinkable and horrific things. She was born in Eastern Europe where she lived on a farm and had to work for everything—food, water, clothing, shelter, the basics of life. That was a time when you worked hard and kept your head down. You worked hard to just survive.

In her first years, she endured much pain and suffering. When she was eleven years old, the war ended, but she lived as a foster child while her mother was fighting for her life from tuberculous. My mother was rejected by the children of that family. She lived as a refugee and, eventually, as an immigrant, coming to the U.S. in 1951 at seventeen years old. In the States, she took care of her parents until they died in the 1980s. She dealt with sexual assault— hers and her children's— as well as losing a child.

To say she lived a reactive life is an understatement. She did not have the emotional tools to combat all of what happened to her and her family. Her survival instinct took over and she lived in a state of fear with a need to control her surroundings.

PART 3: How I Lived My Life

There was a big age gap between my next older sibling and me, so I always felt like a tagalong. I had a feeling that I was an afterthought in my family, like they thought, "Oh yeah, remember her?" I felt like my parents lived their lives with me in the background like they were thinking, "Oh yeah, remember? We have another one." My mother signed me up for several different activities to free up her time, to be away from me, at least that is what I thought and felt. Or I was her constant companion, not able to leave her side. I always felt underlying fear. All of this combined led to me forming the belief I lived with for years: everyone is more important than me.

I lived with criticism that wore on me and I always needed validation. I constantly doubted myself and felt that I should not make decisions. This led to me being very reactive, accepting what was happening to me, and never taking charge of my own life. The thought of speaking up and saying what I was thinking never occurred to me. What did any of that matter? I was not important enough. I just wanted to be accepted. I would try so hard to be part of a group, but I was constantly rejected. Sometimes, I wouldn't even allow myself to get to that point. I would self-sabotage so the rejection wouldn't hurt so bad.

When I was in fifth grade, about nine or ten years old, my group of girlfriends at the time decided that I had done something to warrant being shunned. The shunning would have been bad enough, but some girls took it upon themselves to bully me with harassing phone calls and outwardly mocking me at lunch and recess. Pretty much any time they could, they would bully me. Our group was the most popular in elementary school, if there is such a thing at that age. This went on for the rest of the school year. This was something that I tackled on my own. My family did not know that anything was wrong or that I was in any form of distress. After summer vacation, things seemed to go back to normal. I never did find out why the shunning happened or what I supposedly did, but that feeling still lives on, always surfacing when I least expect it.

Situations like that caused me a lot of stress. Another big trigger came from an episode when I was twelve. I had just come back from camp and my entire room was packed up. I was informed that my mom, sister, and I were moving to Utah to live with my oldest sister who was attending Utah State University at the time. For a twelve-year-old girl on the cusp of junior high, this was devastating. I cannot tell you if I said goodbye to anyone, including my father. Off we went across the country. We only stayed in Utah for seven months. My parents got back together, and just as I was getting used to living in Utah, back East we went. I spent the rest of my high school days finding my place and trying to fit in but never feeling that I did.

Do you remember the fish bowl? I struggled to get out of that small bowl. As a teenager, I grew "too big for my britches." As I moved to another bowl, all the emotions followed me, but I didn't have the tools to put them in their place.

I was diagnosed with alopecia areata around age thirteen or fourteen. This autoimmune disorder causes patches of hair loss. Let's be honest—it was another stressor in my life.

I learned to live small, to not be noticed, to play it safe. Living in my small fish bowl had served me well. My pain, discomfort, and suffering were minimized when I lived on autopilot—not making waves or putting myself out there. I played it safe.

That also meant not trying new things, learning, or growing. There can be no growth without being uncomfortable first. I wasn't happy but I was safe, for the most part. If I did happen to get a crack in my fishbowl or step out of my "zone," self-doubt would creep in and I would self-sabotage again. My days were filled with mindless tasks and procrastination. If I didn't try, then it wouldn't hurt as much when I was rejected because I didn't really put in any effort.

My own family took the brunt of my emotional dysregulation. There were many episodes of lashing out—yelling followed by the silent treatment or manipulation. I have so much guilt associated with raising my children and treating them this way, and also for teaching them these ways of coping with emotions. My sweet husband would sit and take my yelling during a disagreement and just say, "What else?" It used to infuriate me! Now I realize that I just wanted to be heard and have my feelings validated.

PART 4: Awakening

Life was passing me by. I could see outside of my fishbowl and I yearned to be a part of things—anything really. I craved connection with anyone and everyone. A fabulous friend was inspired and sent me to a couple of local retreats. There I found that I was not the only one who felt this way. I was buoyed up as well as terrified. Old patterns never die!

As one does nowadays, I happened upon some social media profiles that started my quest to wake up. I guess at that point, I realized that I was in that fishbowl. Do you remember the movie *The Truman Show*? Truman didn't know it was all fake! I can relate. I didn't know I was not living my life to the fullest. On these newfound profiles, I learned about "inner child" and "ego" and what those mean, and how they affected all that I did.

My inner child was screaming for help. She needed to be loved, recognized, validated, and comforted. My ego was protecting me, but never letting me truly live. It does what is familiar and safe. I realized I was not able to reach my potential, whatever that was. I also realized that I was never just me. I was always that girl who was trying to fit in and be loved. One can't have connections while constantly adjusting who they are. I wanted to be my authentic, true self. If I was a terrible person, then at least I would be authentically terrible. I wanted to be accepted for who I am, not what I bring to the table. (I do bring a lot to the table, though!)

This is a frightening process. The perspective I gained was so eye-opening. At times it was sobering and shameful, but other moments were cleansing and hopeful. The intense feeling of joy and sorrow would be so overwhelming at times that all I could do was just sit with the emotions and let them flow through me.

I started to journal, but not in the normal way. I would find quotes or references and I would write them down to see how they fit into my life or my values. Sometimes they would fit in and other times they wouldn't, but that didn't really matter. I was finally being authentic and connecting to those who felt the same way I felt.

When I began to awaken, I could not allow myself to say yes or even no, but I had the power of choice. This was very empowering! I was taking charge of myself. I was #1 and still am!

I recently had an epiphany that helped me to learn more about how to take charge of myself. I had asked my husband to do some things for me. As I saw him doing other things but not what I had asked for, I found myself slipping into those thoughts, "I'm an afterthought to him. I'm not important enough to get what I asked for or needed from him." But then I realized that I had made myself an afterthought *to myself*. So I worked through those feelings. How could I be an afterthought to myself? How did I make my life work that way? And then the breakthrough: If I'm an afterthought to myself, then others will think that way and feel that way about me because I am *allowing* it. I can be confident but not valuing myself if I'm *choosing* to make myself the afterthought. I should not be an afterthought for myself. I should be number one! That's *my* self-worth, *my* value! I am important just because I am here.

Self-care has become a priority for me. I do my self-care to keep the limiting beliefs and negative thoughts at bay.

Some examples of my self-care are:

- Sleeping enough, being consistent (ish) with bed and wake times
- Intuitive eating
- Cold therapy

- Saunas
- Setting boundaries with others and myself
- Moving my body constantly
- Choosing empowerment
- Embracing ME
- Acting instead of being acted upon
- Dance therapy
- Meditations

PART 5: Moving Forward with Hope

I strive for connections. I am not interested in the surface anymore. Don't get me wrong, I can still talk small, but the deep connection is where it's at. These connections are in order of priority for me.

1. Self
2. God
3. Husband
4. Children
5. Extended family
6. Friends
7. Others

Without a connection with myself, the other connections cannot and will not thrive! For me, connection with myself looks like setting boundaries and saying "no" when the guilt response is "yes." It looks like learning, listening to my body and my spirit, moving my body, and having time to be alone. To have healthy connections with myself and others, I try to see myself and others for WHO they are, not WHAT they are. When you embrace not only who you are but who you can be (or your potential)—that is power.

The Dig Method taught me to take the negative thoughts and limiting beliefs and turn them around. It started as a slow process, but soon I realized that I could get out of the negative spiral faster than before. Changing my thoughts is becoming automatic.

There is hope. Your thoughts are not facts—they are not set in stone. You and I have the power to replace them with hope, light, and love. We need to do this so as not to live a life filled with fear and doubt.

Fear and doubt stop us from progressing, from becoming who we are meant to be. Fear is not true—it's a lie! I have recently uncovered five fears—five lies—that have slowed my growth and sometimes stopped me from living bigger and being who I'm meant to be.

1. Fear stops me from talking to people. Fear tells me, "They don't want to hear what you have to say. You're not important. They will just reject you."

2. Fear tells me that I'm an imposter, that I shouldn't try to learn or grow, because I can't be as good as anybody else.

3. Fear has told me that I can't express what I feel because what I feel is wrong.

4. Fear tells me that if I love too much or with everything I have, that love will not be reciprocated. Those I love will reject my love, just like the high school boyfriend I poured all my love into who rejected my love and forgot all about me. Fear tells me that I will relive that experience if I put all of myself and my love out there.

5. Fear tells me that I can't be who I am here to be because it's too much; I'm not ready for it and I should just stay in my place. Fear makes me ask, "Why should I want more?"

Fear and doubt have kept me stagnate for too many years. Fear has held me back from everything I have wanted to do. Everyone has fear, but it's just an obstacle to overcome. The other side of that obstacle is amazing. Bringing fears into the light diminishes their darkness.

We are children of God, the Divine, the light—whatever you want to call it—but we all have intrinsic value. We are loved, even when (or especially when) we don't value and love ourselves. Hope is not lost! Even a glimmer of light brings hope. You have to start somewhere and where you are right now is as good a place as any. "By small and simple things, great things come to pass." So take action. Do something to move you toward that glimmer.

You are not alone in these washing machines of emotions. Everyone has them to some degree; they just are not talked about. Silence is Satan's tool. He wants to isolate us. There is strength in numbers and community. We are not meant to be alone in this world.

Growth is messy, painful, and overwhelming at times. It is a roller coaster, but there is no growth in comfort or ease. You will never reach your potential staying in that fishbowl. Strength comes from vulnerability, fear, and rejection.

My mother suffered and passed on the pain. It wasn't her plan, but it helped me find my purpose. My purpose is to share and help others—to be a voice. I have gratitude for her and love her for fulfilling her purpose, for accepting that sacrifice for a higher cause.

As Brené Brown said, "Because true belonging only happens when we present our authentic, imperfect selves to the world, our sense of belonging can never be greater than our level of self-acceptance."

That self-acceptance can come from realizing that you are just the right amount. You are not too much. You are not too small. Don't be too small. You don't have to fit into whatever mold others try to put you in. Remember that you are important, just because you are here. You are not an afterthought. You are the very first thought.

2

MORE THAN ENOUGH

By DeAnn Barney Clinger

For most of my life, when I would think about myself as a little girl, I couldn't picture her face. All I could see was a small silhouette. I wasn't sure why. I wasn't even sure that it mattered.

But now I know why. And I know that yes, it does matter.

The truth is that until recently, I never truly knew or understood "little me." I didn't think that little girl had much to offer. I didn't see all of her the way I see her now. It's taken a long time for me to really see her—for me to be able to picture her innocent face and recognize just how beautiful she truly is. I've fought through broken relationships, heart wrenching loss, crippling insecurity, and even addiction to get to where I am now.

But now, I can honestly say I love that little girl I once was. Because of that, I can love the woman I am now.

And because of *that,* I know that everything I've been through has been worth it.

***

I grew up in a large family, a family I am very proud of. I was surrounded by loving parents and grandparents, incredible siblings, and countless aunts, uncles, and cousins, most of whom were always loving and supportive.

I was rarely alone, but I often felt lonely.

I'm the oldest daughter of ten children. Every one of my siblings is smart and gifted with obvious outward talents: playing the piano, singing, dancing. One brother is a musician. Two of my brothers are attorneys. I have one sister who went to hair school and the others all finished college. They have all started successful businesses. Every sibling is witty and naturally funny. They are amazing spouses, parents, and friends.

It's easy to brag about them, but growing up, I couldn't help but compare myself to them. It seemed everything came easily to them, while I could never see what my gifts were. I really struggled in school. I would overhear the conversations my teachers had with my mom, saying I just didn't understand the things I was supposed to be learning. I tried so hard, but I just couldn't grasp certain concepts. I didn't realize until later in my life that I had a learning disability (in the 70s, those things weren't talked about). I tried the flute and the violin and took piano and dance lessons until I was about fourteen. But I never excelled at any of it. I got through school by the skin of my teeth.

I had plenty of adult role models to look up to but my Grandma, Clarene Barney, had the most profound impact on my life. She was my absolute favorite person. She was everything that is good in the world: loving, patient, gracious, and kind. She saw me for me—as an individual, not just as "one of ten kids." She made sure I felt loved and special, and when I was with her, my insecurities didn't seem to matter so much. My biggest fear was that she would pass away. I remember taking naps with her. She would always fall asleep first, and I could hear her quiet heartbeat. When the air conditioner would kick on, I'd wait for it to go off so I could hear her heart beating again. I felt so safe with her.

Of her five children, my dad was her only son. He inherited a lot of her wonderful qualities. He was large in stature but as tenderhearted as could be. For most of my life, I thought my dad was close to perfect. I remember the first time someone told me that it was okay for my dad to not be perfect. I was confused by what they meant because, to me, he was.

And then there was my mom. She has always been one of my biggest cheerleaders. I know she loves me fiercely, but as a child and young woman, I didn't always feel that. She was raising a lot of kids and only had so much energy to go around. As a child, I just felt I was in the way and that I didn't matter. I had ideas of what I wanted our relationship to look like and was disheartened when the reality didn't live up to the expectation.

As I look back on these people who helped raise me, I can see them for who they are: imperfect people trying to do the best they could with their own challenges and situations.

Of course, little DeAnn didn't have that perspective. All I knew was that I never felt quite good enough. I was insecure about my height, my weight, my grades, and my talents (or lack thereof) compared to those of my siblings and friends

All that insecurity made it hard to see the real me.

Looking back, I laugh at myself. I look at pictures and, yes, I was tall, but I wasn't the big girl I thought that I was. Those things didn't matter and should not have defined me as a person, but they were instrumental in who I thought I was and how I made choices for many years to come. If I knew then what I know now, I would have done things differently and been a little kinder to myself.

Going to high school and growing up in the 1980s was the coolest thing to me. I had the best time in school. I loved my friends, I loved clothes, and I loved all kinds of music, especially alternative rock. I was a typical teenager, but deep down, I struggled with feeling that I was different from my siblings and my friends. In my eyes, they were doing everything the right way—the way that would make my parents proud. My friends didn't seem to struggle with grades. Why was it easier for the others? Why couldn't I just *get* it?

I seemed to get in more trouble and I always got caught. My brothers and I always joke now about getting in trouble and having to go sit in the motorhome bathroom when traveling together as a family. I love that we can laugh about it, but back then, it felt like I was again the one getting in trouble for not doing things the right way.

I continued to look down on myself. I never felt I was good enough. I thought often about when I would be happy. I thought I'd be happy when I graduated high school. I thought I'd be happy when I went away to college and became a "real" adult. And more than anything, I just *knew* I would be happy when I got married and became a mother. I'd find an amazing man like my dad—someone who was patient, adoring, and who loved me unconditionally. He would give me confidence and strength. That's what marriage was, right?

Plus, all I really ever wanted to be was a mom. It was my biggest dream. I loved kids and I loved my big family.

If I could, I'd go back and hug that teenager and tell her that she was okay. No, she was better than okay. I would tell her that she was great just the way she was and that she had nothing to prove. I'd tell her to just be herself. So what if school didn't come easy? God has other things in store for you. Be happy and be kind. Don't wait for a husband and kids to make you happy. Make yourself happy.

If only I'd been able to tell her those things.

I graduated high school in 1988 and spent the next few years bouncing around Idaho and Utah, trying a couple different colleges and careers. I had a generally good experience, even if I was the Arizona girl wearing flip flops and no jacket in -15-degree weather.

Not long after my brother, Denny, returned home from his mission in 1991, he and I moved to Utah where I started attending Utah Valley Community College, he started at BYU. It was there that he introduced me to Mark, his friend and former missionary companion.

Mark checked all the boxes, the most important of which was that he was a returned missionary who could take me to the temple to be married (the ultimate goal of young girls in my religion). He and I hit it off quickly. From the beginning, it felt different with him than it did with other guys I dated. We dated for three months, got engaged in March, and were married in June.

I was twenty-one, and everything was going according to plan. I had a husband who was going to *complete* me and make me happy. He'd be the one to help save me. I didn't have to worry about feeling insecure anymore.

Except . . . I did. I still felt insecure.

We hadn't been married long before I received a very lengthy letter from a childhood acquaintance of my husband. They told me my husband deserved better and that I needed to change. They told me how wonderful their childhood had been, and how I'd never be able to recreate that happiness or give him what he needed.

I believed them.

That letter really hurt. While this story isn't about all the ugly details of what exactly went wrong in our marriage, I will say that we were two very imperfect people trying to create a life together, and while there were some really good moments, it was still hard.

We had challenges as individuals and challenges as a couple. We had a baby, then twin babies, and then another baby after that. I loved being pregnant and I loved being a mom. Four kids ages three and under didn't exactly take the stress off of my marriage.

We tried to make things work. We saw counselors, and I sought help from my dad, who loved us and wanted to help us work everything out. But I still felt like I didn't have any tools to help me handle my problems. I had no idea how to fix my marriage, how to deal with my insecurity, or how to be the kind of mother I always dreamed of being. In a word, I was stuck.

I made choices that caused pain, which led to other choices that caused more pain. And then the guilt and shame kicked in, and everything quickly snowballed into a situation I didn't know how to deal with. At some point, I shut down and decided I couldn't do it anymore. I lost myself to pain and unfulfilled expectations. I knew who I thought I should be, but I thought there was no hope of ever becoming her.

It was then that addiction entered my life. Addiction was something I didn't really understand at the time, even though it ran in my family. I didn't think it could really affect me. But that was before I knew the depths of pain I could reach. I felt like all was lost, and I was so desperately sad about what my life had become. I'd made all the right choices, and I was still in unbearable pain. So, when someone introduced me to something that would numb me from that pain, that would help me escape what I was going through (even if it was an artificial escape), I fell hard into an addiction that lasted for a couple years.

It was a scary time for my family and me. I was too embarrassed to ask for help. I told myself I could figure it out on my own. I hid myself away, thinking it wouldn't affect anyone, but all that did was separate me from the people I loved the most.

It felt like I was on the outside of a giant bubble, and inside were all the people I loved. My family, friends, kids—they were all inside the bubble, making good choices and doing things the "right way," and it was working for them. They were happy. But I was outside, alone. And even worse, I was there because I had put myself there. My own choices kept me on the outside looking in.

During this time, I got pregnant with my fifth child, which of course took all my fears to a whole new level. I tried to work through it and to do things the "right way." My husband and I were at our lowest point, but still trying to figure things out for the sake of our kids. I was in and out of my addiction, struggling to leave it behind for the sake of my baby and my family.

I did all I could for the sake of this baby girl. I put a lot of hope in her too. If she could just get to us safely, my kids would be happier, I would be happier, and maybe even the dynamic in my marriage would shift. She would be a spot of sweetness in a difficult time.

I hit the forty-week mark in my pregnancy. My baby was going to be born on June 7, 2005, a Tuesday. On Sunday, June 5, I realized I hadn't felt her move very much. I rested a lot and just tried to make it to my appointment on Monday morning, when we would make sure that everything was ready for delivery the following day.

My mom drove me to the appointment. I told her on the way over that I was worried something was wrong with the baby. She assured me I'd be okay, and my nerves would be calmed once my doctor heard the heartbeat. We arrived and they took me right back to the room.

A nurse came in and started to listen for the heartbeat. Nothing. She tried again. Still nothing. She had me adjust my position on the bed, and then called in other nurses to help her locate a heartbeat. No one could find one. We were all very still, and inside, I began to panic. I looked to my mom for comfort. I wanted her to say it would be okay. But she already knew, and I did too. It was too late.

They rushed me to the hospital next door for an emergency ultrasound. They could tell right away that our baby girl didn't have a heartbeat. She was gone.

I couldn't bear it. I sobbed and sobbed. The pain was too much. The medical team decided to put me under until the next morning when they would deliver our little girl. The morning I was supposed to deliver her, I woke up in a panic. I couldn't stop crying. The nurses had to hold me down and the doctors ultimately decided to put me under again.

When I woke up after the delivery, I had already been transferred to my room. The first thing I saw were my sweet children. My heart broke again. This miracle they'd all hoped for had been taken away from them, from all of us.

We named our daughter Ella Elyse. Elyse is my sister Kimberly's middle name. Their birthdays are one day apart from each other. She was absolutely beautiful, with lots of curly hair and beautiful full lips. She was perfect! We were told her umbilical was kinked and wrapped tightly around her arm three times.

I got to spend a lot of quiet time with Ella. My kids got to hold her. My family came to visit. I felt so much love. But I was in such deep, horrible pain.

The next few days were really difficult. My friend Lisa was there to help me with the changes my body was going through after the delivery. The physical pain was difficult, as it always is after childbirth, but what hurt the most was watching my little family suffer. We had dreamed of this little girl coming to our home. She was going to make things better. And she was gone. We had a graveside service for her. It was beautiful.

The following weeks were dark and sad. My parents and siblings went to Hawaii. I felt so alone. I slept a lot, trying to escape the pain. I remember thinking about the women in my life that I knew that lost babies. I wanted to tell them I was sorry for not being there for them.

Once again, I felt like I had failed. Was losing Ella a punishment for my poor choices? I felt so much guilt and shame in those days. And once again, I had no idea how to help myself get through it.

I knew it was time to move on, but it was so hard. I didn't want to do it, but my kids needed me.

The addiction returned. I convinced myself that it was helping me, elevating me to a level where I could function and get out of bed in the morning, where I didn't feel like I had to be asleep to escape. It made me think I could cope.

I was wrong.

For four months, I spiraled into the darkest pain. I wanted to disappear. I was in a really bad place. My loved ones couldn't emotionally reach me. They begged me to get help. I was scared but I didn't want help.

I couldn't face what I was going through. I didn't have the tools to get me through it in a healthy way. It felt like I would never get to the other side. It felt impossible to work through such deep sorrow.

On October 10 of that year, my mom's birthday, I got a call from a dear friend and my sister-in-law. They said, "Let's go. We're going to get you some help."

For whatever reason, that was what I needed. I was ready to face the change I knew was necessary for me to get better.

They both took me to the airport where someone was waiting to take me to Utah. I went to a treatment center where there were others who were struggling like I was.

It was one of the hardest decisions in my life, but it ended up being one of the best as well. Getting my life back on track wasn't easy. Life's problems didn't just go away, even though I had committed to positive change. But I had a purpose, and I knew I needed to fight for myself and my children.

After leaving the treatment center, I worked on building my inner strength. I attended church recovery meetings. I worked on not falling back into the hole I had been in previously. I tried hard to keep my chin up. It wasn't easy, but I made it through.

If it wasn't for the love and hope of my family, I wouldn't be where I am today.

Mark and I finalized our divorce in June 2006. It was both scary and healing. Even though I had come so far, I still felt like the broken little girl I'd always imagined myself to be. I didn't know how to move past that. I didn't know how to see myself in any other way.

At least, not yet. The months following my divorce, I spent a lot of time with my children. It was going to be the new normal for us. It wasn't easy. I dated a little bit, but I knew I needed to work on myself. On September 10, 2006, I went on my first date with Kade. It was an idyllic romance. We dated for two years and were married on October 3, 2008. I was so grateful that I'd gotten a second chance, so grateful that I had a whole new opportunity to do things better. I believed that things were going to be different with him.

There was just one small problem: I still thought I needed him, my husband, to be the source of my happiness. I got married thinking that he would heal my broken parts. Now that I had the right person by my side, I thought I would feel better. I would become everything I wanted to become.

But the hardships kept coming. My dad—the strong, healthy one who I thought was supposed to outlive all of us—passed away just three months after Kade and I were married. Our brother-in-law

Drummer passed away, and three months later, my sister Kimberly (Drummer's wife), at the age of thirty-five, succumbed to complications with her diabetes, leaving behind two young boys.

I would sometimes shame myself for the choices I had made when I was younger. I beat myself up for them, often. I knew deep down that God had forgiven me, but I couldn't't forgive myself.

Navigating life in a new marriage was full of many changes. It was my second marriage and Kade's first, and we both brought our own expectations and weaknesses to the table. We have two incredible and handsome sons together. These boys were absolute miracles for us. I'm grateful for them every day.

The turning point was when Kade and I bought a new home. We found a big, gorgeous house in a family-friendly neighborhood with tree-lined streets and white picket fences. It checked all our boxes, including being near family. I loved everything about it.

*This just had to be it. This had to be what I was waiting for. When we moved in, I just knew that this was the thing that was **finally** going to solve my problems, complete the puzzle, and make me feel happy.*

If you hadn't guessed yet, things didn't work out that way.

It didn't take long for me to realize that the new house didn't bring the new beginning I was so desperately hoping for. The problems didn't go away. The sadness didn't get any lighter. I was still struggling. I recognized some of the same feelings and thought patterns I had had in my previous years, before things started getting really bad. I knew that it would be very easy for me to slip back to a place of darkness, escape, and hiding.

Something about that experience represented the final straw for me. I finally saw it: marriage didn't fix everything, motherhood didn't fix everything, a beautiful house didn't fix everything. Even my religion didn't fix everything. And the unhealthy habits and thoughts I'd tried in the past certainly didn't help.

So what would help? What would fix me? What would help me feel loved, and accepted, and "good enough" for the incredible people I'd been blessed to have in my life?

The answer came, simple and straightforward: the only thing that could help me was me.

I realized that no one knew better for me than I did. I saw that sacrificing myself for others wasn't serving anyone (least of all me). I needed to try something different—for the sake of my husband, kids, and family—but also because I deserved it. Because I needed it. Because I had to be my own hero.

I knew that, in the past, I simply didn't have the tools I needed to deal with life's hardships in a healthy way. So I went looking for them.

It was about this same time that my sister Jennifer developed The Dig, a program that helps people free themselves from trauma and live happier, fuller lives. She had classes and The Dig training that taught us to challenge our thoughts and to understand why we do the things we do.

It was in those classes that I finally found what I'd been looking for. It was there that I heard the stories of countless other women who had been through almost every type of tragedy or loss imaginable. There, I didn't feel alone. And as we shared our stories and applied the tools, we experienced life-changing breakthroughs.

I learned that I can see things differently. I learned that thoughts are not facts. I learned that I am not defined by my mistakes.

And I learned that I am worthy of love.

The Dig and healing sessions with Jennifer allowed me to connect with that little version of me, the one I couldn't see clearly. Maybe she just needed to feel heard, valued, and understood. Maybe little me needed empathy and compassion, especially when she (I) least seemed to deserve it. Maybe little me needed a safe place to share her feelings without being minimized or dismissed. Maybe little me needed to know that she (I) was loved no matter what.

When I look back on my life, it's not hard for me to see the people who loved me. I see my brother Jason holding my hand in the hospital after I lost Ella. I see my grandmother's chest rising and falling as we napped together. I see my dad telling me how much he loved me, and reassuring me that everything was going to be okay, no matter what I was going through. I see all the incredible women in my life who have become my biggest cheerleaders and supporters.

The list of people who love me has always been long. The difference is now, I'm on the list too.

I can finally see the face of that beautiful, little, blonde-haired, brown-eyed girl with a big smile. She was kind! She was smart! She was loving and fun! She wasn't in the way. She wanted others to be happy.

I love her now. I love that little girl who struggled to find her place in her family and in the world. I love the teenager who just wanted to grow up. I love the young married woman who just wanted to please everyone. I love the mother who felt like she had to turn to something dangerous in order to escape her pain.

And I love me, the woman who has gone through it all, fought like hell, and come out the other side.

I've been clean for over 17 years now. Life hasn't necessarily gotten easier, but I know how to handle it. I know how to be present for my kids, how to stand up for myself and my needs, and how to keep myself from spiraling when something hard happens.

There will be people that can't be happy when I'm happy. There will be others who judge me for my past mistakes. There will be those who think I'm annoying or in the way. I won't be for everyone, but at least I know that I'm trying to be better. I'm willing to change what's not working in my life. There is always room for growth, compromise, and forgiveness. No matter what I do, I'm worthy of love.

It's taken a lifetime for me to believe these things. But what matters is that I believe them now.

I love myself. And in the end, that's really all I need.

I am more than enough.

3

THE INVISIBLE GIRL

By Monya Williams

My mom and my birth father married very young because they were deeply in love; my mom was still a teenager, and she was very naïve. Early in their marriage, a relative came to visit and asked who had been smoking marijuana, but Mom didn't know what marijuana was. Together, they searched the house, found my birth father's stash, and flushed it. When my birth father arrived home and learned what my mother had done, he didn't get angry. He didn't want to disappoint my mom, so he promised never to use marijuana again. That was the depth of his love for her.

My mom was a nurse and worked long hours. When I was three years old, she came home from her shift one night to find my birth father passed out drunk or high on the couch. I was sitting against a wall crying and holding my ear with my hand full of blood. She rushed me to the emergency room, where the doctor told her that someone or something had struck my head and caused my eardrum to break. Nobody was at home that night but my birth father and me. When my mom asked my birthfather what happened, he claimed he was too drunk to remember. I suffered hearing loss in that ear and would have ten surgeries on that ear before I turned thirteen.

Because I was so young, I didn't remember that night, and my mother didn't talk about it; I never felt I needed to forgive my birth father. I was grateful for her grace in how she handled that situation. When I was a teenager, I asked her what had happened. She told me the story my birthfather told her was that I was playing around with the ironing board, and he asked me to stop. When I didn't, and it fell over, he slapped his massive hand across the head. Mom told me that no one was certain about precisely what happened but that he loved me and had never hit her or anyone.

My mom and my birth father eventually divorced, and my mom married a Baptist minister. I remember one visit with my birth father when I was seven. I was so excited to see him that I ran into his arms and felt warm and comforted as he held me on his lap and ran his fingers through my hair. During that visit, my birth father decided to give me the nickname "Bonbon." When I asked what Bonbon meant, he told me that a bonbon was a candy that was white on the inside and that my hair reminded him of the color of the inside of that candy. I've carried that nickname my entire life. Even now, my grandkids call me Bonbon.

My birth father was the oldest son and had eight brothers and sisters. I wouldn't see my birth father again for many years. Besides seeing my birth father's sister Nana a few times, I didn't see any of my aunts, uncles, or cousins during my childhood. This lack of interaction with them and with my birth father created deep feelings of abandonment within me. I always felt that my birth father's family hated me, but I never knew why. When I was fifteen, I asked my mom why I never saw my birth father; the stepdad interrupted and said that my birth father didn't want me and that he (the stepdad) was my father now. I wasn't satisfied with that answer. So sometime later, when the stepdad wasn't home, I asked my mom why I didn't ever get to see my birth father and why I never saw his family. My mom informed me that the birth father was in a maximum-security prison and had been for many years. She also couldn't tell me why my birth father's family had not reached out to me or tried to be part of my life, but she did tell me that she never kept me from them. That conversation left me feeling very confused.

When I was eighteen, I surprisingly saw my birth father at a relative's house. He greeted me hesitantly but warmly, and as soon as he wrapped his arms around me, my heart melted, and I remembered how it felt to be in his arms, safe and protected. As good as it felt to be in his arms again, I feared that my mom and the stepdad would find out I had seen my birth father. There was a tug-of-war going on in my heart. I wasn't sure where my loyalty *should* lie. I suddenly felt loyal to the stepdad because my birth father would be gone at the end of the day, and I wouldn't be calling him "dad." I wasn't wrong. It would be several more years before I would hear from my birth father again.

I was married when I got another call from my birth father. He called and asked to borrow $500. My husband transferred the money to him, and I angrily asked him why he would do that and that I knew we would never see that money again. My husband responded that my birth father was family and that we help family when they need it. The next time I heard from my birth father (a few years after loaning him money), he called and asked if he could come to visit. I made dinner, and we waited hours, but he never showed up. Again, I was disappointed by him. At that time, I closed a door in my heart and decided I would never allow myself to be hurt by him again.

But a few years later, when my birth father called and asked about my children and wanted to know when their birthdays were, my heart softened a little. He apologized for hurting me. I told him I had forgiven him many years before and had always hoped he would be in my life again one day. That call made me feel we had a chance at a relationship, but then he vanished again, and the feelings of rejection and abandonment surged through my veins.

In my last two interactions with my birth father, my broken heart was angry, and I told him off both times. As an adult, I wanted to see my grandmother, she lived in a small town, and I wanted my children to know her. We made a tradition of visiting over the fourth of July weekend. I overheard my birth father ask my grandmother why "Monya and her children" never stay with him. When my grandmother didn't respond, I heard him tell her, "Monya just thinks she's better than me." That made my blood boil, and I charged into the kitchen and informed my birth father that I didn't think I was better than him; I *knew* I was better than him. I told him my children were the greatest gift in my life and that I would never abandon them the way he had left me. I told him I had driven by his house the night before and saw that he didn't have a roof on his home, and on the front porch, marijuana was growing in potted hanging baskets. After that incident, my grandmother shared her version of how awful I had been, and my birth father's family further ostracized me.

My last interaction with my birth father was when he was in jail again. I decided to visit him. The building was old and ran down. A guard took me to my birth father's cell. The only way I could talk to him was through a portal; the guards passed food to him through. He began the conversation by saying, "Hello sweetheart, why are you here? I don't want you to see me like this." I asked him, "Do you think I want to see you like this?" He immediately started making excuses for why he was in jail, how it was everyone else's fault. I interrupted him and told him I was sick of his excuses. I told him that he knew nothing about being a father. Through my tears, I continued telling him I prayed day and night through my childhood and teen years that he would come and rescue me. I let him know that he was missing out on beautiful grandchildren. Then I left him with this question, "Have you ever thought about how I feel?" Without allowing him to answer, I walked away and prayed I would never think of him again.

All those times, I prayed that he would come to rescue me; what was it I needed saving from? The stepdad. The stepdad legally adopted me when I was eight years old, and as we walked out of the courthouse the day the adoption was finalized, the stepdad looked at me and said, "Now I own you." Though I didn't know what that meant, I did know that the tone in his voice did not feel good. Because my mom seemed so happy, I never told her what I thought about the stepdad. The changes in my little world started on that day. I would soon learn how very controlling the stepdad was.

When my baby brother was born, I was so happy. I loved him dearly. I thought having a new baby would calm the anger in the stepdad. Unfortunately, he got meaner and more controlling. He stood in the doorway when I showered and watched me. The stepdad said I had to leave the door open because closing it would "cause mold on the walls." It was humiliating. He also wouldn't let me shut my bedroom door, so I dressed in my closet.

The stepdad abused me in every way, mentally, physically, and sexually. I wondered where my birth father was and why he wasn't protecting me from the creepy stepdad.

My spiritual saving grace was attending primary (a church program for children ages three to twelve.) Although my mom was not active in the Church of Jesus Christ of Latter-day Saints, she wanted me to go and participate. I loved how I felt in primary. I loved the songs we sang and the lessons we learned about Jesus. I decided to be baptized when I was ten years old. I thought being faithful and showing Heavenly Father my love for him would protect me from the stepdad's abuse, but it didn't. However, my mom started attending Sunday services with me and was eventually asked to be a youth leader.

Not long after, the stepdad decided to take missionary lessons to learn about the beliefs of our church. He chose to be baptized. It wasn't long before the stepdad started serving in a high-level leadership role. People at church loved him. Anytime he spoke from the pulpit and testified of Christ and His Atonement, it made me sick. For many years, I wondered if the Atonement was meant for the stepdad too. He was contradictory in his actions. In front of church members, he would act faithful and holy, but at home, it was a different story.

At school, I was mocked because I was deaf in one ear. I daydreamed during class and stared out the windows, hoping for someone to love me. When I felt that when the teachers and my mom gave up on me, I gave up on me too, and I became the invisible girl.

Because I didn't trust men, I didn't date very much. I felt vulnerable and insecure about my worth in God's eyes and the eyes of everyone around me. When I first met Eric, I wouldn't say I experienced "love at first sight," but I did experience an energy that pulled me toward him. During our years of dating, I fell deeper in love with him and his family. The first time I met his mother, I was entranced by her Caribbean-blue eyes and beautiful smile. She hugged and held me tightly like she had known me for years. She made me feel loved. Viola was the first person to say "I love you" to me. I loved having a mother figure who taught me to serve others and be happy about even the smallest things in life. She is the humblest person I have ever met. Eric's family taught me how healthy families interact. They played games together, laughed together, and prayed for one another. I always felt safe and comfortable in their home.

Viola was diagnosed with breast cancer. When cancer overwhelmed her body, she asked me to prepare her son for her death. Viola knew it would be hard for Eric to let her go and thought I was the one to help him through that transition. *She never complained and gracefully taught us all the importance of gratitude.*

When she was in the hospital, and it was clear that she would not live much longer, I tried to talk to Eric, but he became angry and asked me to leave if I couldn't be positive. She died that night with her family and me surrounding her with our love.

After Viola passed, I struggled with past traumas and didn't know how to navigate them. I felt empty without Viola and had a massive hole in my heart. It was difficult for Eric and me to come to terms with Viola not living long enough to be at our wedding, so we decided to postpone allowing time for grieving. Eight months after Viola passed away, my little brother passed away. He was only fifteen years old. My parents were out of town, and I was the last person to talk to him. I blamed myself for years for not taking him to the emergency room.

The night he died, we had a house full of members from the church, neighbors, and my little brother's friends. I slipped away from all the chaos into a quiet room to kneel and pray, but the words wouldn't come. I didn't know what to ask for or what to say. Suddenly I felt a tranquil, calm feeling come over me. I could feel my brother's hand on mine and hear him say, as clearly as if he were standing next to me, "I love you. I am where I am supposed to be. This was not your fault. Now you need to move on with your life and be happy." I always promised my brother I would never leave him in that toxic home and that I would stay until he was old enough to move out. He was letting me know it was ok for me to move out and move on. A couple of months after my brother passed away, I moved into my apartment. I finally felt freedom for the first time in my life. Being released from those prison walls was empowering.

Three years after Viola died, Eric and I finally married. It seemed like such a short time later that I found myself the mother of four children under six. I never told Eric about the abuse I had suffered from the stepdad, so he was startled one night when I was triggered by something while he was playing with our daughter. I grabbed her and my son, screamed at my husband to get out, and accused him of abusing our children. Then, Eric learned I had experienced severe trauma, and I realized I needed to face my past finally. I started by meeting with my bishop (leader of my local church congregation) every week. Those meetings went on for a year. The bishop asked if I was ready to face the stepdad every week. I wasn't.

During that year, I started sharing some of the control and dysfunction I lived with Eric. He didn't believe in therapists and wanted to help "fix" me. But when I talked to him about minor things I went through, he would get so angry and could not believe what I had endured. I knew I would never be able to share all the details. He hated the stepdad and my mom for allowing things to happen. Sharing too much with Eric would not be healthy for our marriage. So I finally began seeing a therapist I felt comfortable with.

The therapist invited me to join a private group with six other women, which he thought would help me. In the first session, I was introduced, then the women went around the circle sharing what they felt comfortable sharing. Their stories brought me to tears. I was the last to share. I spoke with no emotion and shared in the third person, saying things like, "The girl's father hit her across the head, causing her eardrum to break." or "The stepdad took the little girl by the hand and led her into his bed." When I finished my story, the other women cried, and they hugged me. I didn't understand why they were crying. Then the therapist told me that the abuse I had endured was the worst he'd ever heard of; I lowered my head and felt ashamed. The stepdad programmed me to feel ugly and of no worth. Then the therapist told me I referred to myself in the third person when discussing my trauma for the previous eight months in our private therapy sessions. The therapist assured me that I was safe and that the pain I suffered as a child had prevented me from being emotional about what I had experienced. I realize now that it was easier to deal with the pain if I detached from it and told it like a story of another girl from a long time ago. I worked with that therapist for another year, trying to connect with that little girl inside of me. When my therapist passed away after a year of therapy, I didn't feel healed, and I was worried.

I eventually felt ready to face the stepdad. I told my husband I was prepared to ask the stepdad why he hurt me, and I asked Eric if he would be with me. We set up a time for the stepdad to come to our house and asked that he come without my mother (I hoped it would be easier for the stepdad to admit what he did without my mom there.) He hugged me when he arrived at our home, and I was stiff. The stench of his cologne triggered me, and I couldn't move. Eric immediately noticed the fear in my face and took me by the hand as we moved into the living room.

When I asked the stepdad why he had mistreated me, he acted confused and didn't know what I was talking about. I determined that he was either lying or had a severe brain problem. As I recounted some details, the stepdad stared over my head at a photo of my little brother hanging on the wall. Then the stepdad nonchalantly mused, "Now I wonder if I ever did anything to your brother." I felt like a bomb was about to detonate in my head. He had been very physically abusive to my brother! When the stepdad asked me what I wanted him to "do about it," I boldly told him to go home, tell my mom about everything, then go see his bishop and start the repentance process. The stepdad *did* go home and tell my mom a big lie. My mom called a week later to accuse me of trying to start drama, and then she said that if I couldn't have a relationship with my "dad," she couldn't have a relationship with me. We didn't speak for seventeen years after that. The next time we spoke was when the stepdad died. She yelled at me, called me names, and blamed me for "everything." I hoped we could heal our hearts and move forward, but that didn't happen.

For years, I felt shame for "breaking" our family apart. I believe that keeping secrets inside me for so long caused breast cancer when I was forty-six. After all, I had been through, I thought my "trial" in life was over. So when the doctor told me I had breast cancer, I didn't believe him. I lived in shock and denial for months and didn't shed a tear. After seeking a second and third opinion, Eric decided I needed to be at The Mayo Clinic. I was grateful for his insistence because they found more malignant lumps. I had two different types of breast cancer and three lumps.

I ended up in surgery for a bilateral mastectomy.

After recovering in the hospital for a few days, the surgeon delivered more bad news: my lymph nodes were full of cancer cells. I would be having more surgery. I started to feel guilty, and the reality of death invaded my thoughts. I asked Eric if I had been a good enough mom. He assured me that, while no parent is perfect, we had done our best with our children. I was depressed. I felt guilty and angry, knowing I would not be healthy enough to enjoy our youngest daughter's senior year of Highschool.

During chemo, I would lie on the bathroom floor throwing up but holding a picture of my grandson and praying to God to take my pain away. When I finally finished chemo and radiation, I was ready to move on with my life! But the following year, I had to have a hysterectomy. It triggered me when my gynecology oncologist explained the surgery. I told my surgeon I was sexually abused and that the stepdad always said, "When I'm done with you, no man will ever want you, and no doctor will ever be able to fix you." After the abuse I had experienced, I was terrified to think of being under anesthesia while the doctor worked on me. My sweet surgeon reassured me that I was in a safe place and that I could trust him.

After the hysterectomy, I still thought about cancer all the time. My oncologist told me that was normal and encouraged me to try to do something I loved every day. He suggested I volunteer and spend time with friends. My children had all grown and moved out, and I tried to be with friends, but I still felt lonely.

A few years after the hysterectomy, my ear started dripping black gunk. When I saw an ENT at the Mayo Clinic, he asked how I'd lost my hearing. I told him I knew about the injury from when I was three and that I'd had ten surgeries on that ear. He examined me and scheduled surgery to clean out my ear and see what was happening inside. After the surgery, the ear didn't get better. Every time the doctor scraped the dead, black skin out of my ear, the ear would fill with blood again, making it difficult for him to know what was happening.

My surgeon talked to colleagues at Mayo Clinic and other ENT friends he had outside Mayo, trying to devise a plan. I was awoken one night by a pop I felt in my head. It was excruciating pain. I didn't want to wake Eric, so I suffered through the night, and then the next day, after my husband left for work, I went to The Mayo Clinic to see the doctor. When I arrived, the nurse looked at me and realized something was terribly wrong. The doctor admitted me to the hospital immediately. I looked like I was having a stroke or Bell's Palsy. I stayed in the ICU for three weeks and endured three more surgeries.

Before I was released to go home, the surgeon tried to explain my diagnosis. He showed us a picture of the tumor he removed and the dead nerve controlling my face's right side. The nerve was black, and it was impossible to bring a dead nerve back to life. The doctor told my husband and me that I would never smile again. I remember him saying the word permanent, and I was devastated.

During one of my surgeries, I coded and had to be resuscitated. It was during that surgery I had an experience where I believed I was in Heaven. I was greeted by Eric's parents Viola and Ray. When Viola hugged me, I felt a peace that was hard to explain. They looked younger, but she still had those Caribbean blue eyes. She was the best person I've ever known. I could not believe I was in Heaven with her. I felt that if I was in Heaven with her, I must have done something good to deserve to be there, and I didn't want to go back to earth.

Viola took me by the hand and told me God wanted her to say that I had a mission to complete on earth and that it wasn't my time yet. She said I needed to go back to earth and tell my story because there were people who needed to hear it. When I opened my eyes in recovery, I asked, "Am I alive?" The sweet nurse said, "Yes, sweetie, you are alive." Learning that my prognosis was permanent facial paralysis and that I would never smile again. I wanted to die. I knew my life would never be the same. The experience I had with Vi and Ray I kept to myself for a long time. I didn't know how I would ever be able to share my story, and I didn't think anyone would believe me.

When I returned home from the hospital, I wanted to return to Heaven and be with Viola and Ray, where it was safe and calm, and I'd have my smile back. I was introduced to a trauma surgeon at Mayo Clinic. He always makes me feel like there is hope. I trust and love him. Before each surgery, I call out his name, wait for his response, and say, "I love you." Not counting the surgeries I had in elementary school, I have had close to 48 surgeries since my cancer diagnosis. Most of them have been with this trauma surgeon. He is my hero and now a friend whom I can confide in. He's always had such sincere empathy for me, he has seen me cry more times than I can count, but I have never left his office or a phone call where I didn't feel important to him, no matter what the world thought of my disfigured face.

Permanent facial paralysis changed me. I hated what I saw in the mirror. I prayed day and night for a miracle. I didn't realize how much it had changed me until my children confronted me and told me I needed to change or they would have to take a permanent break from me. Months passed with no contact, or when I did text them, there was no response. Being unable to talk to my girls or see my grandchildren was the worst punishment I have ever felt. I honestly didn't know what they wanted me to change. I always thought I was a good mom and supported them in everything they did. I just didn't understand where this anger they had for me came from. My heart was shattered into a million pieces; I would never want to hurt or offend them. I prayed for them day and night. I became very sad, lonely, and full of fear.

I became suicidal, and when my attempt to take my life failed, I was admitted to a hospital for mental health. All they wanted to do was give me drugs. That was not what I needed. I took a lot of my anger out on my husband. I didn't believe him when he said, "You look beautiful." How could he love me when I was so hideous, with the scars on my face and my inability to smile? I spent the next few years trying to figure out why I *felt* like I did. I loved my children, but they told me they needed time to heal. I was losing the relationships I thought I had with them. I felt ugly and disgusting. All I wanted was for people, including my children, to acknowledge how hard it was to know I'd never smile again. Instead, all I heard from them was, "I don't see anything wrong with your face." It hurt me to listen to my children say things like that. I knew what I looked like when I looked in the mirror.

My husband and I started going to therapy together. It helped us as a couple, but I knew I needed something to help me work on myself. I recalled something a transformational therapist trained in me. He taught me about the paradigm between our thoughts, what we believe is true and what the facts are. He taught me to be open to new ways of thinking and always to stay connected to God-Energy or the Universe (or whatever higher power we believed in). What I learned from him would help me find what I needed for healing. People who feel unworthy or afraid have a hard time feeling love because fear blocks the feeling and effects of love. The most significant forgiveness we can experience is forgiving ourselves; it's important to have gratitude every day, and that gratitude was part of my healing.

I remember he taught me that I have choices, that I have the power to accept responsibility for how I react to things, and that I have the option to allow myself grace for mistakes I have made. With these lessons in my mind and heart, I sought a way to forgive and heal myself. I realized that I had carried dysfunction inside me from childhood into adulthood, and I knew it was time to get that poison out of my system. I worked to remove the limiting views I had of myself and replace those views with facts. I *had* hurt my children because I wasn't available the way they needed me to be available. I didn't hurt them on purpose, but I could recognize that the shield I had put around my heart had become a barrier to being emotionally available to my children.

After doing my healing work for a while, one of my daughters reached out and asked if we could talk. I was able to *hear* the pain I had caused her. I took responsibility for what I had done to cause her pain, and I realized that we both wanted the same things but didn't know how to communicate those things with each other. My children just wanted me to be a *mom* to them. I didn't realize their feelings when I told them about my breast cancer. I remember thinking that some of my children didn't care because I didn't feel empathy from them. I was wrong. They worried about me, just as I had worried about them, but we didn't know how to communicate that to each other. We didn't know how to connect without offending.

Once I stopped being a victim and listened with my heart, I could feel their worries and see their lives through their eyes. We have come a long way in our healing. I've learned that each of my children is living their journey, with their struggles crucial for their individual growth. Instead of lumping them together as "the girls," I see them as individuals with their thoughts, personalities, and feelings independent of one another.

I have learned that serving others helps me to heal and live in the light.

When you end the state of being a victim and choose to go out and help others, your life can shift from surviving to thriving. When I made this mind shift, I decided I would do something for someone else every day for 365 days. Some days I would leave a kind note for someone. Several times I held open a door for someone. One time I noticed a young mother in the grocery store struggling with her little ones while she shopped, so I offered to help with her little ones, and I went through the grocery store with her and her children.

One day I was driving past a park known for having homeless people living. I counted twenty-six men gathered in one area. I went to a local food establishment and bought burgers and fries for all the men. I happened to be reading a book about the power of positivity, and the main message was that if you do something good every day, good things will come to you, and that will become who you are as a person. I told the men I wanted to read this book and promised them I would come every Wednesday at 4:00 pm.

It was August in Arizona, and the monsoon season was beginning. One Wednesday, it was raining hard, and I thought about not going, but instead, I went to a dollar store and bought umbrellas for all the men who were still attending my reading time. After six weeks of reading to the men, I finished the book, and only three men were left. I gave them baby wipes and told them to clean up and that I would pick them up on Friday to help them find jobs. I took one man to Walmart, and he got a job. They gave him bus tickets to get to and from work until he could get on his feet. Another man I took to McDonald's, and he got a job. The third man I took to Goodwill got the job and is now a manager living at home with his family and has been sober for a couple of years. The other two men live in shelters instead of in the park. I have seen two of them recently, and they are still employed.

This may seem like a really "big" act of service and out of reach for some. But I acted on inspiration to help others. It wasn't hard, and I felt good because I knew I was helping people in need. I started keeping a "warm-fuzzy" jar. Whenever someone did something kind for me, or whenever I did something kind for someone else, I would put a fuzzy pom-pom ball into the jar. It reminds me of the kindness that exists and that I am part of that kindness in the world. Little acts of kindness can change you. When you do something for someone else, it becomes part of you. Those 365 days of kind acts changed me and became a part of who I am today.

Throughout my journey, I have kept a blog. I have a vast audience. What I have shared on my blog has focused a lot on what I see in the world, what I have seen in the Mayo Clinic, photos of procedure rooms, and often how I have felt going into and out of procedures. About a month after the experience I had with Viola telling me to tell my story, and while the facial paralysis was still something new I was dealing with, I was contacted by the CEO of a beauty company. She asked me to come and speak to some of their clientele. I immediately thought, how could I talk to people in the beauty industry when I didn't feel beautiful? I imagined there wouldn't be many people in attendance. When I asked why she wanted me to speak, she referenced my blog and told me that their company wanted people to know what I had been through and that I don't give up.

When I arrived at the San Jose Conference Center and stepped out onto the stage, I learned that there were 20,000 people in attendance and thousands more watching online from home. I felt exposed and vulnerable. I spoke about being diagnosed with cancer and its effect on my family. I told them about the tumor that killed the nerve that controls the right side of my face and how *challenging it has been to move forward in life.*

The message I shared with those people was that no matter how difficult my life was, every day, I told myself to get up out of bed. To do the things I needed to get done, and served at least one person a day, then told myself to do the same tomorrow. I explained to the audience that if they would do the same thing—ask themselves to get out of bed, pray, each day, and serve others when they can. Eventually, they would find that they are not just surviving through their challenges but *thriving through them.* When I returned home, I had thousands of messages on Facebook Messenger. One lady mentioned facing tough challenges and had gone to the conference because friends had invited her. When I started speaking, this woman was going to leave the room, and her friend told her to stay. This brave woman told me she had been planning to take her own life, but after hearing my message, she felt courageous enough to live through her challenges and do the hard things that were before her.

This was the message God asked Viola to share with me to touch just one life. Sharing your experiences and your light doesn't have to come in the form of a speech in front of 20,000 people or a blog with millions of followers. When you feel inspired to share your story and your hope, don't hesitate to share it. Let yourself come out of the dark and into the light. Bringing forward feelings that have kept you in the dark and dealing with those feelings will help you find the light. Forgiving yourself and others allow you to feel the light's warmth. Doing kind things for people invites them into the light alongside you. Give yourself the gift of living in the light. Let your light shine! I know you have the power within you to do so.

Unbreakable

4

EMERGING INTO LIGHT

By Jennifer Fagergren

My first "aha" moment of learning how powerful thoughts are and how my thoughts weren't serving me came when I was twenty-one years old and serving a church mission in Scotland. It was the first time in my life that I remember having thoughts of comparison and negative self-talk. I began comparing my weaknesses to everyone else's strengths. At that point in my life, I wasn't aware that I had the agency to act for myself and control my thoughts and feelings. I thought they controlled me, and I spiraled down fast and hard.

I kept these thoughts and feelings to myself, and over the following few months, I struggled. I had never felt so low in my life. On the outside, everything seemed fine—my companions and I were having success in our missionary work—but inside, I didn't feel like myself. I felt like I was dead. I was numb to emotions and unable to feel the Spirit of the Lord. I felt that, because of this, I couldn't be a good missionary. I felt hopeless and fell into such a deep, dark depression that I didn't want to live anymore. I didn't reach out for help because I felt shame and embarrassment, so I suffered alone.

After much heartfelt prayer, I think the Lord knew that I wasn't going to reach out for earthly help and that He was all I had, so miraculously, He saw fit to help me see the connection between my thoughts and my feelings. He enabled me to change the thoughts that weren't serving me into thoughts that served me better. This empowered me to rise above the dark clouds that overshadowed me and I was freed from this darkness of depression for the remainder of my mission. Whenever I would experience negative self-talk or thoughts of comparison, I would realize that those thoughts weren't truth and that they were not from God. This realization lifted that heaviness I had felt. I had so much growth and became such a better missionary after going through this experience as the Lord helped me see that the adversary was trying to destroy me with my thoughts. Satan was trying to keep me from growing and receiving more light and truth.

Have you ever felt this? Like the adversary was trying to destroy you with your thoughts? I think we all have. Whenever we're about to do something that will improve our lives or that will bless the lives of others, we meet resistance. Certainly, starting to understand how powerful thoughts are and grasping the idea of the importance of developing skills that would change limiting thoughts into empowering beliefs is a blessing, so no wonder I was experiencing opposition. Little did I know that I would continue to struggle with thoughts of comparison, negative self-talk, and feelings of depression throughout my life. Only, the connection between how powerful thoughts are and how my thoughts weren't serving me wouldn't always be as clear as it was when I was a missionary. My mission was kind of like a "Heads up," "Watch out," and "Be aware of what's about to come."

Later, I came to realize that it wasn't just during my mission that I had encountered faulty thinking patterns. As I looked back through the years, I began to see that unhealthy thinking habits were part of my life starting in my childhood years. I was four-years old when my brothers, who were six and seven, accidentally set the field across from our house on fire. They told me to run back to our house as fast as I could to get help. I did, and as soon as I walked through the front door and told my mom, I passed out. That would be the first of many fainting episodes that I would experience throughout my life. When these moments occurred, it was always a response to something that seemed dangerous, scary, or upsetting to me. I think passing out became my coping mechanism for these emotions. I see now, though, that these feelings were triggered by faulty thinking habits and patterns that I actually had control over, although I didn't realize this at the time.

Throughout the years, I went to many doctors but never received a diagnosis in relation to my fainting episodes. Now that I have learned about emotional resilience and have developed some self-coaching skills, I know what to do when I'm experiencing these kinds of thoughts and emotions. For example, the last time I had to get my blood drawn, which had always triggered me to faint in the past, I used breathing and meditation tools along with affirmations to help me get through it without passing out. Also, in the middle of a church meeting recently, I felt the sensation that I was going to faint. My old, ingrained thinking patterns came to the surface. "I'm in the front of the chapel. Everyone's going to see me. This is going to be so embarrassing. I don't want to disturb the meeting." I felt the need to pass out so strongly right there and then, as if I had no control. Well, after reading those thoughts I was having, do you think those thoughts made the situation I was in get better or worse? You probably guessed it right. It got worse fast. My palms were getting sweaty, my heart was racing, and I stopped breathing (all signs that I'm about to pass out). Before my emotional resilience coaching training, I would've passed out—no doubt about it. This time, however, I became aware of my thoughts and the feelings in my body. I had the tools to become the observer and I knew I needed to take deep breaths and change my thoughts that weren't serving me, so I did. I started to think, "Oh, yeah, I see that my palms are getting sweaty and that my heart is racing, but that's okay. Everything is going to be okay. These feelings in my body will only last for ninety seconds and then they will go away. I'm okay feeling these emotions until they leave my body. They're just uncomfortable, but they're not going to hurt me." Soon, all feelings and sensations of passing out completely went away and I felt as if everything was back to normal.

Do you see the contrast in the different thinking patterns? I was able to change the thoughts that would've led me to pass out into thoughts that served me and my body better. I've come to realize how much my thoughts have influenced the fainting episodes throughout my life. All along, I believed it was just my body's reaction to danger and fear and that I had no control. Now, I've come to understand that I do have control. I had been giving my power and my agency up, but I have the ability to act for myself and to choose my thoughts. I'm starting to believe that, for me, passing out was a form of a panic attack. All along, I allowed the thoughts in my brain to lead to feelings of fear, danger, and worry and these feelings took over my body, which led to it shutting down. Now, I have the tools to stop the panic right in its tracks before it turns into an attack where I've lost all control. The emotional resilience coaching tools and skills that I've learned have helped me not only live my life more free of panic and worry, but also to heal the trauma and pain in my life.

After my mission, I fell in love with a West Point cadet and married him, not knowing at the time that we'd spend the next twenty years in the military service. We had four kids, moved fourteen times within twenty-one years (with two of those moves being overseas), and went through two Afghanistan deployments. In his first deployment, my husband worked with an infantry team that was embedded with the Afghan army. I was home alone with our kids, trying to hold down the fort, when something happened to me unexpectedly that has left me with trauma and PTSD that has reared its ugly head off and on ever since.

The reality is, life is difficult for everyone. We each have hard things that happen to us. Life is stressful and messy. We're all on a journey to live out our own individual stories. I've come to learn that having a tendency for perfectionism, being a people pleaser, and engaging in negative self-talk and thoughts of comparison, combined with feelings of overwhelm and stress, is a recipe for disaster when you lack emotional resilience habits and tools. Trust me, I know this all too well.

Six years ago, when our family was living in Brazil, we were holding a family scripture study that turned out to be an utter disaster. I lost my patience, yelled at my kids and husband, then left the house feeling discouraged and depressed. My thoughts and feelings spiraled so low that I remember feeling like I wanted to drive my car off of the JK Bridge. I felt that my husband and kids would be better off if I just quietly disappeared. Compare that to now. We still have stressful family scripture study at times and experience other "utter disaster" moments, but now, with the emotional resilience tools and habits I've been implementing, I'm more able to change the story and see things differently. I take deep breaths. I meditate. I do some thought work, asking myself questions like, "Is it really true that I'm the worst mom and wife ever?" Then, whether I think it's true or not, I ask myself, "Is this belief serving me?" The answer is always no. I also ask myself, "What outcome do I really want?" In this case, I wanted peace and healthy and happy relationships with my husband and kids. These thought-provoking questions that I ask myself help me to change limiting thoughts and beliefs into thoughts that empower me and lead me closer to the outcome that I really want.

I've learned to practice self-love and self-care, have self-compassion, and forgive myself and others. Doing these things enables me to hold the space needed to create instead of react. It helps me to show up as my best self for myself and others, which helps my relationships improve. I'm still working on these habits though, and recently, there was another family upset similar to the one we experienced six years ago in Brazil. Again, I lost my patience. I needed to be alone, so I drove away, only this time I implemented the emotional resilience skills that I've been working on. Thanks to these tools, I didn't spiral down fast and hard like I did before. And this time, there were no suicidal thoughts, so to me, that's a big win!

Another recent win for me was when I was in the middle of an emotional resilience coaching program and our family moved from Texas to Arizona. Out of our fourteen moves, this move was by far the smoothest transition for me emotionally and it was even during a pandemic. I chalk up this success to my practice of meditating, journaling by doing thought-work to change limiting beliefs into thoughts that serve me better, and practicing self-love and self-care.

Our kids missed their Texas friends so much that the only summer vacation they wanted to take was to go back to Texas to see their friends, so that's what we did. I loved seeing them with their friends. I hadn't seen them that happy since before we moved, and I found myself starting to spiral, thinking things like, "Oh, no . . . what have we done? It was hard enough to say goodbye to our friends when we moved, and now we're going to have to say goodbye all over again. We shouldn't have come. We never should have moved." Then this affirmation came to mind, "Everything is how it should be." We should have come to Texas. We should be happy to see good friends and we should be sad to say goodbye to them. We should have moved. Everything is how it should be.

The words we choose to use really matter. God created the world by His words and we create our own world by our words. Words such as "shouldn't have, always, and never" are words that argue against reality, and any time we argue against reality, we lose. Focusing on the past and wishing things had gone differently fosters depression. Focusing on the future with unproductive thoughts fosters anxiety, but living in the present brings peace and joy. Moving that many times with our family and being continually on the go, out of our comfort zones, and in transition hasn't been easy for me emotionally, but I'm thankful to now have tools that make these kinds of transitions less stressful and more manageable.

I mentioned that over my husband's first deployment, something shocking happened to me that caused me to experience trauma and PTSD. This has been the hardest trial I've had to endure up to this point in my life. When he deployed, the kids and I moved to a small town in southern Utah. We rented an older, run-down home. I remember the day that this shocking event occurred. Afterward, I was on my hands and knees, mopping the kitchen floor. The old, ugly linoleum floors were so dirty and cracked. I remember feeling like my world had just turned completely upside down and feeling like my life was just like the floors I was trying to clean: dirty, ugly, cracked, and broken. I was in a mess and didn't know how to fix it. The pain that infiltrated every cell in my body and every ounce of my soul was a certain kind of pain that I never knew existed before. I had never felt this kind of intense pain. This pain not only broke my heart and crushed my spirit and soul, but it made my stomach so sick that I couldn't eat for weeks.

I had a faith crisis, not knowing why God would allow this to happen to me. I eventually turned to God in prayer. I was ANGRY and kept asking WHY? WHY THIS? WHY NOT something else— anything else? I wouldn't wish this upon my worst enemy. I didn't tell a single soul. How could I? I was full of shame and embarrassment. I suddenly felt as though I was forced to isolate myself from everyone and everything, and I hated every second of it. I suffered alone and continued to suffer alone over the following seven years. During this time, the Lord knew I wasn't getting the earthly help I desperately needed, so thankfully, He blessed me with answers to my prayers that brought some relief to my suffering.

While we were living in Virginia, where we had moved after my husband returned home from deployment, I was blessed to have a spiritual experience that brought me strength. I had been feeling very alone in my suffering and was wondering if I'd ever heal. One day, I was praying hard, asking if I'd ever be healed and pleading for some kind of relief in my suffering. Then I let my scriptures fall open. They fell to Alma 15, so I started reading this chapter. Zeezrom had been in his bed, sick with a burning fever and he said that his mind was "exceedingly sore because of his iniquities." When Zeezrom saw Alma and Amulek, he stretched forth his hand and asked them if they would heal him. Alma asked, "Believest thou in the power of Christ unto salvation?" And Zeezrom replied, "Yea, I believe all the words that though hast taught." Alma said, "If though believest in the redemption of Christ, thou canst be healed." And then Alma cried, "O Lord our God, have mercy on this man and heal him according to his faith which is in Christ." I knew this scripture was specifically for me. I knew through the Savior, Jesus Christ, I could be healed.

Another time, while living in Texas, I decided to ask God in prayer if I chose to go through this trial before I came to earth. I said, "Heavenly Father, I know I wouldn't have chosen this." I told myself and Him that there was no way I would have chosen it. I wouldn't have chosen this and the kind of pain it evoked in me in a million years. I wouldn't wish it upon my worst enemy. Then after my prayer, these words came to my mind and heart, "How do you know you didn't choose it?" I knew then that maybe I didn't choose this specific trial, but I did choose to come to a mortal, fallen world, and I did choose to experience the pain associated with living in a place such as this, susceptible to the effects of sin, accidents, death of loved ones, and other heartbreaking circumstances. Because I chose to come here, I'm not immune to any of it. I knew God was aware of me and my pain and I knew He'd be able to heal me. Yet, I knew the Lord didn't want me to suffer alone. God didn't put us on this earth to suffer alone.

Ironically, the first time I reached out for help was while my husband was gone again. It was over his second deployment to Afghanistan. During this time, the trauma and PTSD came back in full force, as if I was reliving the shock and horror of what happened during the first deployment. I would imagine all sorts of violent things happening to me and would be overcome with terror as I imagined them happening. It was the same feeling of terror I had felt before. It was a tough time and I knew I needed help. I needed support. I needed healing. Despite the shame and embarrassment surrounding the circumstance, I was ready to reach out for help because I needed healing in my life. You'd think out of the two of us, while my husband was fighting the war against terrorism, that he'd be the one to experience PTSD. Thankfully, he returned home whole and healthy in every way. That was a blessing. However, I did experience PTSD then and still do from time to time.

Seven years after the first deployment, while in the middle of the second deployment, I reached out to get support from some family members, friends, and others who could support me. I finally started to feel more relief and freedom from my suffering than ever before. I still have false thinking patterns that show up around the circumstances of this event, but now, with the support of others and with the coaching tools I've gained, I'm more able to do the necessary thought work to change the false thinking patterns into true, empowering beliefs that serve me better and free me from the prison I find myself in at times. It seems like whenever I'm about to receive more growth, peace, and light in my life, I'm hit hard with these limiting beliefs. Resistance always finds a way to creep in, but now I know what that looks like and can use my agency to act for myself and do the things I need to do in order to counteract the opposition and to receive the truth, peace, and light I long for. I know that God shows up in our stories when we petition for Him to do so. He has the power and ability to turn our ashes into beauty. He meets us where we're at. He comes and shows up in our messy, dirty, ugly, and broken places because that's the kind of God that He is.

Another time when I was suffering and didn't know how to move forward in my pain, I had fallen to my knees, pleading for help and praying most of the night. Then, I got up and was getting my kids ready for school, packing their lunches, and it was as if letters and numbers had been suddenly etched into my forehead. I saw them so clearly. They read Doctrine and Covenants 123. At the time, I didn't know what this section of scripture was about, but I knew that message came from God, so as soon as I got my kids off to school, I read it. I came to the last verse, which reads, "cheerfully do all things that lie in your power; and then . . . stand still, with the utmost assurance, to see the salvation of God, and for His arm to be revealed." That was the exact instruction I needed. Move forward. Act and do not be acted upon. I knew that through this trial, I had a choice. I could become bitter or I could become better.

I have worked to become better. That doesn't mean that negative self-talk, comparing myself with others, or feelings of depression don't appear in my life. There are three tools I have acquired that I implement every time one of those false thoughts comes up so that I can live my life in more freedom.

1. Ask: "Is this thought true?" and then if it is true, ask, "Even if this thought is true, does it serve me?" Something I

learned from The Dig is, when I have negative thoughts or when one someone else says something that triggers negative thoughts, step back and ask these questions. If the thought doesn't serve me, I can change the thought into one that serves me.

2. Change your state, change your environment, change your energy. One thing I do when negative self-talk, comparison, or depression darken my world, is change what I'm doing. If there is a lot of noise, I remove myself from the noisy environment and seek a quiet place. If there is music playing that is agitating me, I change the music. I move my body. If my body or my environment is dirty, I clean it up. I find a way to change my internal and my environmental state.

3. Use my "Five S's to Serenity." Serenity is the state of being calm, peaceful, and untroubled. The Five S's to Serenity are:

   Stop

   Still

   Shift

   Soften

   Sun (and Son)

When life doesn't feel right, or when I've reacted to a situation poorly and I feel heavy and dark, I remind myself to *stop* and be *still* so I can notice what it is that is causing my reaction. Then I allow my heart to *shift* from hard to *soft*ness so that I can receive the *sun and the Son*. The *sun, and the Son* of God, are the light that heals the heart and allows me to feel lighter and let go of the darkness that has momentarily disrupted my peace.

We all have hard things that happen to us. It's not what happens to us that causes suffering in our lives, it's what we believe about what happens to us that causes the suffering. Elder Jeffery R. Holland said, "A life without problems or limitations or challenges . . . would paradoxically, but in very fact be less rewarding and less enabling than one which confronts—even frequently confronts—difficulty, disappointment, and sorrow." I know this is true. It is because of the pain and sorrow I've experienced that I've been able to experience love and joy and feel truly alive. I know that we need to experience the bitter to know the sweet. It's because of my painful experiences that I've come to know how real God is and how I've learned about the Atonement of Jesus Christ in such a personal way.

We can choose to be thankful for all things. As I chose to focus on the blessings, it made the pain seem purposeful. There is a peace that comes when we choose to be thankful, even in our suffering. I know that we are engraved in the palms of His hands, He who suffered all. Our Savior knows each of our pains and what we have suffered. He suffered the same things, so He could succor us. Elder Jeffery R. Holland said, referring to missionary work (but I think we can relate it to life in general), "I am convinced that missionary work [or life] is not easy because salvation is not a cheap experience. Salvation never was easy, we are The Church of Jesus Christ, this is the truth, and He is our Great Eternal Head. How could we believe it would be easy for us, when it was never, ever easy for Him?" Life wasn't meant to be easy for us, and to tell you the truth, I'm glad. I would've never come to know my Savior, Jesus Christ, in such an intimate way if life was easy. If life were easy, I would've never come to know how real He is through my experiences of receiving answers to my prayers and witnessing His hand and His miracles in my life. Through my experiences of depression, suicidal thoughts, anxiety, panic attacks, relocations and deployments, and trauma and PTSD, I've come to know the love and power of God and the love and power of His son, Jesus Christ. I know they have the power to heal all things. I've also come to know the power of thoughts and the importance of reframing thoughts that aren't serving me. I've learned the importance of self-love, self-compassion, and the power of forgiveness for myself as well as the power of forgiveness for others. My prayer and hope for you is that you will find healing, peace, and freedom in whatever trials life brings to you through God or through whatever higher power you believe in, and through these emotional resilience tools that I've mentioned. You're not alone in your suffering. There is support out there for you. You are loved, my dear friend.

Unbreakable

5

WHEN LIFE GIVES YOU CRAP SANDWICHES

By Jennifer Nielson

Many people feel broken—sometimes. But me? I can't remember a time when I didn't feel that way.

For as long as I can remember, I've felt like something was deeply, inherently wrong with me. But unlike other people who just *thought* they were broken, I had *proof.*

From a very young age, I subconsciously collected evidence that validated my brokenness. I collected these "crap sandwiches" like my mom collected Precious Moments. I filled an invisible curio cabinet with suffering, bad luck, and overall "wrongness." I felt like my every flaw and weakness was on display for the world to see, the crap sandwiches piled so high that no one, not even myself, could see beyond them to the real Jennifer.

My view of my life and the world was skewed (figuratively) by these thoughts, but it was also skewed (literally) by one of the first crap sandwiches life ever handed me, when my eyesight was permanently damaged when I was just two years old.

I had wandered into our neighbor's backyard where my brothers and their friends were playing baseball. Even as a toddler,

I was determined not to miss out on the action. Well, the action found me in the worst way. I was hit directly in the right eye by a baseball, resulting in a detached retina that left me blind in my right eye, with a lazy eye to boot. The doctors hoped that my eye would heal if I laid flat on my back for a month. It didn't.

I came home from the hospital and slowly adapted to life with one eye. It was a huge challenge. My parents would have me wear protective goggles and avoid certain activities to protect my eye. The possibility of going blind was real.

My sister loves to remind me that there's only one "eye" in Jennifer, but all jokes aside, accepting this situation was difficult for me, especially as I grew. I hated that I was different. I hated that I couldn't watch 3D movies with my friends. (Flash forward to a massive letdown at the Captain EO ride with Michael Jackson at Disneyland.) But what I hated most was my lazy eye. It made me feel ugly. It felt like proof that something was seriously wrong with me—proof that was right on my face for everyone to see.

That may have been the first crap sandwich I collected, but it certainly wasn't the last.

At three years old, my friend Jamie and I decided to go swimming at his house. Alone. We stole his sister's Wonder Woman swimsuit (yes, my superhero dreams came true!), suited up, and jumped into the pool. The fun didn't last long, because I couldn't swim. I ended up in the deep end, thrashing my arms and struggling to breathe.

I was drowning.

I only have fragments of this memory, but I do remember reaching for the light—and feeling absolutely terrified. Luckily. Jamie's mom pulled me out of the water to safety. The next thing I remember was being wrapped in a towel and crying in my mom's embrace as she offered me a can of Sprite.

My youthful impulsivity didn't end in tragedy that day, but it made me familiar with the feeling of fighting for my life. It's a feeling that never really left me, and one that added to my sense of brokenness. For other people, life didn't seem like so much of a struggle. But I knew better. I knew that for me, things would always be hard.

Around this time, I was handed one of the biggest crap sandwiches I'd ever get: I began to be sexually abused by my uncle. At the time, I didn't realize how the abuse impacted me, mostly because I was able to dissociate from the experiences and lock those memories away (in fact, they stayed locked away for decades). I'm grateful for that dissociation, because it allowed me to function. But I couldn't rid myself of the feelings the abuse left me with. Unworthiness, shame, people-pleasing, and compulsion for perfectionism were ever-present. I don't remember a version of myself without these unwelcome companions. They showed up in every facet of my life, especially in my relationships.

This was particularly evident in my relationship with my mom. I can remember a journal prompt in first grade that asked, "If you could have one wish granted, what would it be?" My answer was simple: "To make my mom happy." I believed my sole purpose in life was to make her happy. And I tried hard.

I can remember a Mother's Day when something caused my mom extreme distress. She left the house in tears and told us she was never coming back. I watched her from our large picture window in the living room as she drove her blue station wagon out of the cul de sac, unsure if I would ever see her again. Not only was I devastated, but I felt somehow responsible. I believed that if I had behaved better, or helped more, or colored her a nicer Mother's Day card, maybe she would have been happy. Maybe she wouldn't have left. She did return eventually, but that feeling of abandonment reinforced my desire to please. To be good. This was my job. It became my identity.

It also reinforced my "crap sandwich" belief that I wasn't enough. The way I saw it, my job wasn't to just be myself and let others accept and love me. My job was to change, shift, and bend my actions and personality in order to be what other people wanted me to be. "Just me" wasn't good enough.

I kept finding evidence that this was true, and that I was broken. Whether it was being cast as the prince instead of the princess in the neighborhood plays, being called cyclops, or being the last one picked for kickball at recess, there seemed to be more proof everywhere I looked.

There were moments when the grit in me would show up and I would fight back. I remember once in third grade, disappointed after another brutal day at recess, when I told my dad, "I want to buy my own kickball." I was determined not to be the last one picked, and I figured the best way to do this was to create my own team on my terms.

Looking back on moments like that, I can see a spark of something different in me—something a little more confident and a little more ready to stand up for myself. But by far, the more common theme was looking to others to determine my worth and happiness. As a result, my people-pleasing and perfectionism ran my life. They blinded me to my innate goodness and talents. I couldn't see the good in me; only the bad. This plagued me through my awkward junior high years and into high school.

A journal entry from my freshman year speaks volumes. "I'm just not satisfied with myself. I'm so ugly! I have ugly eyes, ugly hair, ugly color of skin, zits, big rings under my eyes, no boobs, long legs, ugly feet and toes, ugly hands, I don't have a shape, and I have a stupid personality. I don't know what to do. I'm really depressed. I'm confused about everything."

I even enlisted God's help to fix me. I would pray desperately for him to make me prettier, smarter, or more confident. Or I'd ask him to help me sing and dance like my sister Stacy. Seriously, was it too much to ask to be able to do the damn splits?

My prayers seemed to go unnoticed. I felt so alone. I felt forgotten. Even after I had surgery to correct my lazy eye, I still struggled to love myself. Like many teenage girls, I was looking for self-love in all the wrong places. I thought if I could be pretty, it would solve all my problems.

Around this time, I read about a pill in the back of the Seventeen magazine called THE PERFECT 10. This pill promised magical results of physical perfection. In desperation, I filled out the order form, wrote a check, and put it in the mailbox with a hope and prayer that my problems would finally be solved. Surprise, surprise: the pills never came. My hopes were dashed.

Throughout high school, I did my best to ignore the crap sandwiches and enjoy what were supposed to be the best years of my life. I hid my self-loathing and despair well. I tried to always be "on," and I did a pretty good job at it. I was voted class clown my senior year, had lots of friends, and did everything I could to hide my secret pain.

I was constantly reminded of how lucky I was. Big family, big house—you get the drift. I even had a teacher who called me "Barney Bucks." Apparently money, a big house, and cute clothes automatically equated to happiness.

Except I wasn't happy.

Underneath the facade, it was brutal being me. I ached deep inside to find acceptance and validation. I lived with shame, anxiety, depression, and deep insecurities, made worse by the fact that I was "supposed" to be grateful for the incredible life I had. But external abundance in any form doesn't equate to internal happiness. This misconception was and is extremely damaging and toxic when you are struggling with shame, depression, and anxiety. Especially as a teenager. The unspoken message to me was, "What does she have to be depressed about?"

But the truth was, I could have lived in a mansion, had all the money in the world, and still felt broken beyond repair.

Those material things were not what I cared about. I just wanted to be loved and liked. But because I thought I was inherently broken and unworthy, I thought I would never get the love and validation I was looking for.

This put me in a constant state of fight or flight. Eventually, I just wanted to disappear. It was too much.

There was, however, something I learned as a teenager that would help me feel just a little bit of the validation I was looking for. That was being liked by boys.

As a natural romantic (I cried at The Little Mermaid as a five-year-old), it didn't take long for me to become boy crazy. The search for romance, companionship, and the ultimate validation became my quest. As you can imagine, that set me up for heartache.

I fell in love with boys in England, California, Utah, Florida, and Arizona. I even won a kissing contest with my friends the summer after I graduated—I kissed 30 boys.

Of course, those boys couldn't fix me. But maybe a *husband* could.

I met Talan at a bowling alley on a big group date. It was infatuation at first sight. He was gorgeous, charming, funny, tan, and recently returned from a church mission. We started dating exclusively soon after. We had fun, we fought, we made out a lot, and within a year, we were married.

Before I became a teenage bride, I had a very clear picture of how married life "should" be, but just days into my marriage, that image began to unravel. Talan wasn't how I thought he "should" be, so I made it my mission to fix him. I took on the role of the fixer in my marriage, just as I had done in my family growing up. The "shoulds" exhausted me. Looking back, they made it impossible for me to be present or feel happiness.

Once again, the thing that was supposed to fix everything had just turned into another crap sandwich—more proof that I couldn't be happy with myself or my life.

Then, about 13 years ago, the motherload of crap sandwiches nearly buried me alive when my dad passed away unexpectedly. My marriage was on the rocks, our home was in foreclosure, my daughter was dealing with debilitating health issues, and I had just suffered three traumatic miscarriages. During this time, I was in my mid-thirties and all the memories of the sexual abuse I'd experienced as a child came flooding back.

All at once.

The evidence I'd been collecting over my lifetime built up into a rock-solid case, proving once and for all that suffering, anxiety, depression, and hopelessness were my life sentence. This was it for me. It was never going to get better, and there was nothing I could do about it. And it didn't seem there was a magic wand powerful enough to fix my broken parts.

In this period of trauma overload, I nearly lost the will to keep fighting. I would fantasize about getting hit by a Mack truck— something to take me out of my misery. Anything was better than the hell I was living in.

To my credit, I tried. I churned through dozens of different counselors, healers, and coaches, searching for The One who could fix me.

I still count it as one of my life's greatest blessings that I actually found him.

The man I refer to as "Stevie Wonder" was a different kind of counselor than what I was used to. While most counselors I'd talked to were gentle or even soft-spoken, Stevie Wonder called me out on my crap. He wasn't unkind about it, but he was direct, and while that wasn't necessarily what I wanted, it was definitely what I needed.

He challenged the "broken" story I'd been telling myself my whole life.

He challenged my belief that I was unfixable.

He told me that I was angry, and that I was repressing my anger (which made me so angry that I wanted to punch him).

And one day, he looked me straight in the eyes and said something that would change my life forever.

"Jennifer," he said, "you don't have to be the victim anymore. You can choose to free yourself."

I mentioned before that I sometimes wanted to be hit by a Mack truck; well, these words hit me like one. They knocked the wind right out of my victim-thinking sails. If I was in control like Stevie Wonder said I was, then all the "evidence" I had of my brokenness was called into question.

I could choose to believe that so-called evidence, but I could also choose *not* to believe it. Realizing that made me feel immediately empowered, a feeling I hadn't really felt before.

The feeling was real, but it was also new and unfamiliar. It didn't take long for me to start questioning it. After all, I had all that evidence! It was so convincing! It was real...wasn't it? I'd been telling myself those crap sandwich stories for so long that trying to set them aside felt like lying to myself.

But I couldn't shake the power of Stevie Wonder's words. They resonated with something deep inside me. They stuck with me long after he spoke them. I remembered them, I repeated them, and I internalized them, until finally, it really clicked.

I had two choices: I could quit, or I could choose to fight for my healing.

I chose to fight.

I began to tap into the power within. I began to regain some hope that I could be healed.

I finally decided to take ownership of my life. I quit "shoulding" all over myself. I fired myself as the "fixer" of everyone else's problems.

It wasn't easy. It took asking for help and doing a lot of work to figure it out. This marked the beginning of a harrowing journey of self-discovery and healing. Part of this journey included pressing charges against my uncle, who had sexually abused me and nearly taken my life as a child. I couldn't dissociate or pretend anymore; I had to face it all. I had to go deep within myself and stir up the pain. I had no control over what happened to me as a child, but as an adult, it was 100% my job to speak my truth, face it head on, and learn to handle it in a healthy, productive way.

Doing this work allowed me to challenge the harmful thoughts and beliefs that my life had instilled in me—not just the childhood abuse, but the personal insecurities, the struggles with my mom, and the hardship in my marriage. Once I took ownership of my own mind, and *chose* how to feel about the hand life dealt me, I was finally free to embrace my life as it was, not how I thought it "should" be.

I went from feeling like I was drowning to a place of thriving. But the real miracle isn't that my uncle was sentenced to 402 years in prison, that my marriage is now rock solid, or that I strengthened my relationships with God, my children, and myself. The triumph is that I could take all the crap sandwiches I had once begrudged and instead use them to help others on their healing journeys to freedom and peace. This has led to more profound healing as I've realized that helping others to heal is the ultimate healing tool.

Now, I truly believe that we all have the power to create our own destinies, no matter how many crap sandwiches we're dealt. The strength I needed to survive and thrive had been there all along, just like Dorothy's ruby slippers had always had the power to carry her home. I believe that strength lies within each of us.

I have faced more than my fair share of struggles, and in the process, I developed resilience, grit, and faith. I came out on the other side stronger, happier, and ready to be the best version of myself.

Now that I'm finally free, I want to help others liberate themselves and discover wholeness. We can all experience peace and fulfillment in our lives, no matter how many crap sandwiches life throws our way.

6

POWER OF PERSEVERANCE

By Roxy Pingree

Panic attack

Alone, balled up in the fetal position, I found myself lying on my closet floor. I was drowning in my own tears, frantically trying to catch my breath. I was suffocating in my fears.

My mind was wracked with overwhelming confusion and desperation. I was silently screaming for help, calling upon my Savior as this wave of thoughts and beliefs flashed through my head. This moment of emotional despair and anxiety was attacking my body. My heart was pounding at record speed, my head spinning so fast I couldn't see straight, all while I was desperately gasping for air.

I had been trying to pull everything together, but the harder I tried, the more chaotic everything became. It was as if all my struggles were conjugating together, conspiring to take me down. I was completely depleted, both physically and emotionally. "I am not going to let them win!" I said to myself while wondering if maybe, in this moment, they were.

The Lord shows up perfectly for us with what we need, not necessarily with what we want.

Without having spoken a word, I knew He heard my pleadings. I had this awareness of my Savior's insurmountable love and compassion for me. I felt as if He was pouring it upon me, as this warm sensation filled every cell of my being. In that moment, I could breathe.

My soul was not only heard, but it was also felt. I knew that He knew my desires and intentions. I received the most generous reassurance that my Savior was pleased with my progress, desires, and abilities. The imperfect me was absolutely enough.

Prior to this panic attack, I was in desperate search for answers and solutions—my world was falling apart. My best efforts hadn't been enough. I was attempting to do the impossible, trying to make sense out of the nonsense that addicts bring with them.

In this moment, I did not receive the answers I had been seeking. Instead, I received a whopping dose of much-needed love, compassion, and reassurance. It was powerful and it was perfect.

The assuring words, "the Lord entrust you" came in with its priceless offerings.

My struggles led to making the Lord my priority

The five years previous to this panic attack had significantly contributed to my anguish. Connecting with the Lord was no longer *just an option* to be fit in when it was convenient. My battles were huge. I knew I couldn't do this on my own if I was going to get through this with any kind of success or sanity. I needed miracles and direction.

Making Him my priority led me to the sweetest relationship with my Savior and accelerated the building of my character. I guess I can thank my despair over my husband for these gifts.

Discomfort drives us to find solutions.
And it requires us to build our character.

Through this process, I have learned just how expansive His offerings are. He came in and gave to me the validation and compassion that my husband had not been capable of offering at that time.

Many of my lowest moments of discouragement simultaneously became some of my sweetest and most elevating experiences with my Savior.

A little bit about my life

Pregnant at seventeen, I married my high school sweetheart. This was not an ideal start, but we absolutely loved each other and we were both determined to prove *we could do this*. By the time I was twenty-four, we had four adorable little boys who gave us a new kind of joy and a wonderful education. At age twenty-six, I was diagnosed with Multiple Sclerosis (MS). Our fifth son would come more than ten years after my MS diagnosis.

The love of my life was amazing in so many ways. He had a way of bringing fun to life. To this day, no one has ever made me laugh and giggle so much. He was full of all kinds of adventure. He was also full of trauma, which he brought with him to our marriage. The longer you avoid dealing with childhood trauma by "numbing out," the more disruptive that trauma is when it manifests in your life. Long story short, he struggled with addictions on and off throughout our marriage.

Anyone who has had a spouse that struggles with addictions understands the impact and burden it puts upon you (the non-addicted spouse). After he had gone to treatment a couple of times, I thought this addiction had finally been put to rest. Unfortunately, it had a way of showing up again, uninvited.

Throughout our life there were struggles in and out and conquered, but this one, for me, was always lurking in the background.

My blessing

"The Lord entrust you" was a Godsend and has become one of my most loved and valuable spiritual power tools gifted to me through a blessing I received. Never have I felt like a blessing was so directly from the Lord. It was personal and contained details that the administrator of the blessing could not have known. There was a certain place in the blessing in which I knew the words before he spoke them. I cannot explain it, but I know the Spirit was generously offering me a second witness to a memory of what my spirit already knew. I remembered not only agreeing to the trials I would face, but also feeling honored that the Lord entrusted me with so much. Oh, how I needed this reminder at this very moment. It was as if the heavens had opened for me for a split second. This memory came down and will be forever imprinted upon my heart.

He understood the complexity of the various challenges I was facing and was offering me a spiritual gem of a power tool. It was multi-faceted in its offerings, motivating and reassuring me in those moments of doubt and despair. His confidence in me invoked a strength in me.

It testified truth to me when the discouragement and exhaustion were pulling at me and shouting at me to convince me otherwise.

We all have our own personal wilderness journey which we alone must walk. He knew He probably shouldn't come in and rescue me from every pain and all my anguish. That would be robbing me of my opportunity to grow and build my character. He gave me something grand and I could choose to take this gift and cherish it. It was an offering which enabled me to show my gratitude for Him each time I pulled it out and applied it.

Time and time again, those priceless words, "the Lord entrust you" have succored me, coming in to disentangle the confusing thoughts that sneak in. This manifested a powerful truth to my limiting thoughts and beliefs, turning my struggles into purpose and my despair into hope. Those words alone continued to refuel me with motivation, confidence, and purpose. His sweet assurance taught me that I am capable.

I share this story because I believe this is true with each of us. The Lord entrusts *you*. What kind of confidence, motivation, and hope would it offer you if you were to apply this truth during your moments of struggle? Knowing there is purpose and that He entrusts you! I know I was not given this spiritual power tool just for my benefit. I was *entrusted* to share this empowering truth with you—that the Lord has confidence in you!

Exhausted—physically and emotionally drained—throughout this healing process, I continued to build upon my relationship with my Savior. He became my dearest friend: my "bestie."

I have come to know Him intimately, which has been one of the greatest gifts my struggles have offered me (and there have been many gifts in these struggles).

Along this exhausting and seemingly-long uphill journey, I have continued to receive these nudgings. Each has been a Godsend, providing a necessary tool to add to my personal character-building.

Had I not received these tools, I would hate to think what direction I may have taken or where I would be. Not only have they sustained me, but they have also helped me navigate the murkiest waters. That's not to say that I have always taken the best paths in my life. I have made mistakes, and those mistakes have exacerbated the pain in my life. But once I turned to and committed my life to Christ, He led me perfectly. When I choose to follow the paths He leads me on, I know I am going the direction He wants me to go and I notice the Godsends in my life.

Unable to share all of my Godsends and power tools within this one chapter, I want to share those that have been the most life-changing and have led me to this place of learning how to be emotionally resilient through the worst of times.

Women's Conference: Sharing my struggles

Sometime after receiving that blessing, I attended a Women's Conference with my dear friend. I was sitting next to her, listening as five women stood up and, one-by-one shared their toughest struggles. One's husband was struggling with addiction. The next woman had struggled with illness. The third woman's husband was jobless. Another woman's house had burned down. And the final woman had a child who struggled with addiction.

As each woman stood up to share, my friend and I would look at each other with this straight sort of smile and raised brows, knowing I could personally relate to each specific story all too well. I understood those struggles because I had experienced those very same struggles.

By the fifth story, we just laughed to ourselves. Then, without thinking, I leaned over to my friend and out of my mouth came, "that's because the Lord entrusts me." She was well aware of where that had come from.

More time to notice and ruminate

As my children grew up, moved out, and started families of their own, I was left with more time and the less energy. I found myself ruminating in conflicting thoughts, trying to make sense out of nonsense. As the MS progressed, my ability to function decreased and I found myself slowly detaching from the social world. Looking back, I probably kept myself too busy and involved when I felt I wasn't making a difference in my marriage. This didn't leave time for me to focus on what I had no control of. This is a place I would find myself when my husband was in addiction mode. With each attempt to address the issues of addiction, I experienced the effects of my physical body "failing" coupled with the emotional effects of my unsuccessful attempts to emotionally connect with my husband.

My struggle with MS

As time has gone on, I have struggled to forge forward with a body that has wanted to stay behind. Throughout these past few years, there have been days when I have just wanted to be "done." Those who know me would be surprised to hear this. The full-of-zest me has felt completely depleted. My body had been deteriorating and attacking my organs. The burning pain has attacked almost every part of my body. The excruciating pains and ailments have been manifesting themselves more often and in more extreme ways. The thought of just getting dressed has sometimes required more than I have to give. The fight has felt insurmountable. For so long I have been determined not to let the MS win but I started to feel like I was fighting a battle that I was losing. Each time I have wondered how much more I could take, the Spirit has shown up big in various ways, offering me a dose of what He knows I need. I haven't always been spared the pain, but each of His offerings has provided me a magical kind of comfort which has made my pain more sweetly bearable.

My greatest pain and trial

Although MS continues to be a huge struggle, it has not been the cause of my greatest pain. My most painful challenge has been watching the man I love struggle with addiction. His brain had been rewired. He was reactive. You see, addiction induces fear and pain. It robs the addict of their self-love, self-control, and logical reasoning. This meant that trying to have a logical conversation regarding his addiction was not an option. Conversations would leave my head spinning as the addict brain would excuse or shift blame to deflect off of him. It felt like nonsense I could not ever make sense of. I would feel my best qualities attacked and at times question myself, wondering if the accusations against me were true. I felt like I was living with a foreigner who was not anything like the husband I knew. I knew and loved his spirit and I understood that this was the addict, however, it was taking its toll on me. The addict's fear of facing their past becomes a delusional fear of truth for them. As a result, they create their own playbook of lies and manipulation to sustain their selfish rules. The self-hatred presents itself in the ugliest of ways to those they love and trust most. I had to set a boundary that I would not engage in conversations with him that didn't involve looking for or finding solutions. That boundary was a power tool and I used it. It kept me safe from the various manipulation tactics, the worst of which was gaslighting. I was no longer available to participate in this dance of lies.

He was looking to escape the pain he had unintentionally caused. It was heartbreaking to see the pain it was causing his soul and not be able to help him.

Brain classes

One of the many nudgings I received was to take some online classes on the brain. The first class covered the addicted brain and how addiction rewires the addict's brain pathways, bypassing the prefrontal cortex functions of reasoning and logic and allowing thoughts and experiences to go straight to the amygdala. The amygdala is responsible for processing strong emotions, such as **fear, pleasure,** and **anger**. When the amygdala is over-stimulated, it is hyper-reactive.

That explained a lot! There's the "nonsense" behaviors I had been trying so hard to understand and make sense of.

The nudges to take the next two classes came at the same time. Those two classes were about the subconscious brain and neurolinguistics. I had no idea what neurolinguistics was. I just recognized the nudge of the Spirit and history had proved it was directing me to something more elevating.

In short, neurolinguistics is the study of how the brain collects and stores our experiences, as well as how the input of those experiences affects us. Scientists have discovered that our brains have the quality of plasticity, which allows us to create powerful change with our input.

The word "subconscious" refers to mental activities that operate in the mind beneath or beyond our conscious awareness. Combine that definition with the (generally accepted) fact that 94–98 % of what we do is directed by our subconscious mind. That sounds like an invitation to self-destruction!

This was clearly something I needed to tap into! I wondered, was I being attacked by my own subconscious mind? I was blown away when I learned about the power of the subconscious mind.

Our brain's job is to protect us. The problem is that our subconscious mind doesn't know the difference between protecting us and interfering with our growth.

Similarities between the subconscious and the Adversary

As I studied the mind, I began to notice similarities between the subconscious mind and how the adversary works on us.

Both gain control of our happiness when we are not aware or when we are not paying attention. They are both sneaky and hurtful . . .

Satan's method is to influence the thoughts of men, tempting them and enticing them. As I pondered, I thought, what better place for the adversary to take advantage of us than in our subconscious mind, where we aren't consciously aware. Wow! What a destructive combination the two can be! It's a perfect setup for self-sabotage, discouragement, doubt, fear . . . all those things that imprison us and generate unnecessary pain. This realization, of course, fueled my incentive to become *more* self-aware.

This was another Godsent power tool I received.

Whenever I feel discouraging thoughts, I recognize the perpetrator of such thoughts: Satan. Recognizing this only motivates me to double my efforts and do the opposite of those thoughts that Satan has planted and to oppose him and his team. In my mind, I'm showing him that first, I recognize him and second, every time he tries to mess with me, I'm more motivated to be better.

The good news that counters the "bad news" of the trouble that can come from the subconscious mind is that we know we have power over both Satan *and* our subconscious minds. From neurolinguistics, we have learned that our brains have the quality of plasticity, which allows us to take control and mold the input we receive to create powerful change. Plus, we have our Savior constantly working on our behalf. He is the greatest super power we have access to.

Don't believe everything you think!

The Spirit will make our conscious brain aware of real danger.

When we don't pay attention, we will find ourselves sitting in a banquet of lies.

We don't have to drink the poison that our limiting beliefs serve.

Understanding the power we have to change our subconscious narrative is not only empowering but necessary, even vital, to our well-being and growth.

This deeper understanding compelled me to put into practice all I had learned about our brains. I consciously started catching and reframing those limiting beliefs. I learned to take a thought or a feeling and ask myself: is this fact or feeling? is this truth or emotion? Whenever I feel uncomfortable, I take that as a nudge to look deeper and find out what is behind that uncomfortable feeling. And once I understand that, I can find ways to reframe that discomfort to serve me better. When we discern between emotion and truth, we can put them in their place and reframe.

I honestly thought that my inner chatter was pretty healthy until I started paying attention and recognizing when it wasn't healthy. Let me just own that delusion. It was quickly squelched by my experiment.

My first experiment recognizing and reframing my subconscious thought

I was just starting to come out of a lengthy and painful exacerbation with my MS. I remember looking down into our family room, my body feeling as if I was carrying hefty weights as I made my way down the stairs. I was tempted to slide down but worried I would break another one of my wimpy bones. I felt overwhelmed at the mess and I heard the thought, "I am never going to be able to be organized like I once was." I'm pretty confident this thought was generated and exaggerated by my body's struggle and lack of cooperation.

Here was my chance! I could put what I had learned to the test.

I immediately thought and actually said out loud to myself, "Seriously Rox! Did you just hear yourself?!" I had caught myself doing the very thing I was relatively convinced I didn't do. Here was my opportunity! I recognized my limiting belief and decided to reframe. I knew that I could not tell my brain something I didn't believe, like "I am going to be organized." That was just pushing it. I decided to reframe my thought and tell myself that each day I was going to *become* more organized. That felt more believable. (Looking back, it felt safe because there was no time line or criteria I had to meet. I could do one thing per day as I was able). So, I literally said out loud, "each day I am going to become more organized." I said it again and it felt right, and that was the end of that internal dialogue.

A week later one of my friends called and said, "You sound out of breath. Are you ok? What are you doing?" I said, "I am on a cleaning roll." She replied, "You must be feeling better! What sparked this?" In that moment, I realized I had completely forgotten about my little experiment. I literally hadn't thought about it again until right then. I was blown away! I had attacked my craft room—the very room I had been avoiding for so long. It had been on my to-do list but every time I walked in, I became so overwhelmed, I would turn around and walk back out. That was just one of the to-do list rooms I had gotten organized. This was super powerful to me. Without giving any more thought to my experiment, I had set myself up to succeed. My brain believed what I told it!

Since this experiment, I have been faithful in following every nudge and have been seeing the rewards of my efforts flow in. I clearly see how each nudge has perfectly prepared me for the next, with each being an extension of the last. The Dig was no exception.

The Dig

A dear friend got me into a Dig retreat at the last minute. I didn't really know much about this retreat I was going to. Here again, the Lord worked through others. I had been praying for direction on what my next step was. Serving others has always been my number one go-to antidote for keeping me from going into a funk. We all need to feel useful, right? With my unpredictable body, I needed to know how I could serve and give back what I had been so generously offered.

The answer was made clear at the Dig retreat. I was to take this life coaching course and help others become emotionally resilient when the hard things come up. What I didn't realize is that as I would work with others, I would continue to experience growth myself. I had been prepared for and safely led to this perfect place for me.

Though I was led to the Dig, it felt like an arrival for me. It was this tidy assembling of all the years of lessons I had learned and practiced along the way. The very power tools I had been led to were included in this retreat. It was organized in a simple yet powerful and productive format. I knew I had been prepared and set up for the Dig.

One of the most valuable quotes for me was:

It's not about what happens to us.
It's about what we tell ourselves about what happens to us.

This is so simply put and offers so much insight. Often, we unknowingly add limiting beliefs to the events in our lives, which causes added grief. I had added myself to my husband's events or choices that had nothing to do with me, yet I always felt like I needed to reassure him or *make* him understand that the stories he told himself were not true and were causing him unnecessary pain. What I didn't realize was that in trying to remove his pain with reassurances, I was neglecting myself—the only person I am ultimately responsible for. In addition, I was doing my husband a disservice by trying to remove the pain he felt—pain that was necessary to move him to action to overcome the addictions that were causing him the pain.

- We cause ourselves unnecessary pain by believing the limiting thoughts our subconscious screams at us.
- Pain is inevitable; suffering is an option.
- We are responsible for our happiness despite what others do.
- We have the power to change the stories we tell ourselves. Becoming more self-aware and recognizing our thoughts enable us to reframe and better serve us.
- We always have a choice.
- Pain can be a motivator in moving us to healthier ways of living.
- Failure is not final. Reassign your "failure file" to a "feedback file."

These valuable truths are simple, yet they reveal so many lessons.

If it isn't serving you and causes you unnecessary pain, it may be your subconscious brain reacting to past experiences and interpretation because it thinks it needs to protect you.

Finding my breakthrough

It has been the most painful challenge to learn about addiction and how it affects the addict's brain and behaviors; to learn to recognize the effects of my husband's addictions on me; to not take his behaviors personally; to become more self-aware of my own subconscious thoughts and reframe those thoughts to serve me; and to understand that my husband's addiction is not about me and it is not my job to "fix" it. I would have to say that it has only been possible to deal with this most painful challenge in my life because I have yoked myself with Christ and felt His peace and love. Christ has given me truth and support throughout my journey. I have been divinely led. There is purpose to our struggles. They motivate growth and build our character. My hardest hard times have been filled with reassurance that He loves me and that what I am doing is enough. His love is never withheld because of my lack. He fills in for my lack. He loves me in all my imperfections.

Something else that has helped me to deal with the craziness that I've had in my life with a spouse struggling with addiction has been finding a support group for wives of addicted spouses. I had a friend who introduced me to one of her friends who she knew was dealing with some difficult things. My friend thought maybe her friend and I might have a few difficult things in common and be able to help each other. I went to lunch with my friend's friend and within minutes we discovered that we were both married to men who struggled with addiction. We share all of the same effects of addiction—lying, gaslighting, blame-shifting—all the things that make a person feel like they are going crazy. It felt good to not feel alone. It felt good to feel validated. I again felt like the Divine was guiding my life to bring me to another person who helped me take the next step in my healing.

Together, my new friend and I got brave and started attending a support group. At first, I felt a bit apprehensive that someone might see me going into the meeting and judge me or my husband. It took all of five minutes to quickly realize that this support group was there to help me and that what I think of me is most important. Participating in that support group was the beginning of my breakthrough. It was validating, educational, spiritual, and empowering. These truly were some of the most amazing women going through hard things—cancer, grief for death of loved ones (including the loss of a child), grief for wayward children, health ailments—and yet every one of them said that the pain and sorrow of dealing with their husbands' addictions was the most agonizing of all their trials. From our shared experiences, we all gained strength. They were truly all warrior women. Any woman who has gone through the birthing experience knows that it is a hard struggle and there is a lot of pain and discomfort involved, but then she gets to the beautiful—a beautiful she would never give back. Through that pain she discovers a strength she didn't know she had.

With each new struggle, a new kind of strength emerges.

Learning about addictions was essential for me. I took the online brain classes. You may feel like there are other ways to understand addiction and in so doing, find a way to escape the carousel of crazy that your loved one's addiction puts you on.

Hope

Had I not gone through this painful journey, I would not have learned the valuable lessons I have learned, nor (do I believe) would I have developed the relationship I have with my Savior. If I am being honest with myself, I probably would have been "too busy" to commit to the time I do. All along, I knew I could thank my husband for giving me the purpose I needed for me to commit to the time.

When you walk with Christ, you will always reach your destination. Your Divine destination.

As I have committed the time, I have come to know Him, trust Him, and love Him in the sweetest, most intimate way. I have always believed in God and have been grateful for my Savior's sacrifice; however, these very painful trials have taken my understanding and appreciation to a whole new level. I knew He was by my side and that not only was He aware of me, but He also knew my pain. This knowledge brought me closer to Christ as I gained a deeper appreciation for His sacrifice. My pain wasn't even a smidgen of what He went through. How can we possibly begin to relate to or appreciate His sacrifice for us without experiencing a tiny spec of the pain that made Him who He is?

God did not remove Christ's pain and suffering, because it was important for Christ to know how to be with us in our suffering. I knew that *He* knew not only my physical pain but also my emotional pain. Minutes prior to my panic attack, my supplications to my Savior were for answers and direction. The Lord did not give me what I asked for; instead, He gave me what I needed. He showed up for me in my moment of trauma and validated me. He has been involved in my decisions, has guided my direction, and has turned my surviving back into thriving in a new kind of way. I have become emotionally resilient to the toughest of things.

Christ generously gives us exactly what we need to be successful, when we are ready to receive.

Christ won't remove our pain and suffering, because that act would rob us of our purposeful and very personal growth and the opportunity to build of our character. What Christ *will* do is be with us, strengthen us, and help us as we grow through our struggles.

I had been desperately trying to pick up the pieces of my shattered heart only to have them yanked out again. When I gave Him the pieces, He healed my heart by solidifying the pieces together in a beautiful way, making my heart more resilient. He is the perfect friend everyone would benefit from inviting into their lives. I will forever treasure our time together. He's not an option. He's a priority.

He knows our strengths better than we do. Looking back, I can say His timing is always right—not easy, but right—and necessary for our becoming. Our struggles can define us or we can choose to let them refine us. We get to choose. I consciously and consistently chose to turn to Him, learn of Him, and follow Him more diligently than ever before.

I chose to put all my trust and faith in Him. The more I studied his life, the more gratitude, admiration, and love I felt for Him. It's not possible to *know* Him and not love Him. It's the sweetest of all kinds of love. It was Him that I could fully trust. He speaks truth and I needed wisdom and sure direction.

I am forever grateful for the many beautiful and amazing friends and the support groups who have brought much support, wisdom, and love into our forever friendships. They truly were an important part of my healing. We can read books and take all kinds of classes, which is wonderful. Knowledge truly is power. Christ gave me everything that I specifically needed for my circumstance and growth. Without a doubt, those friends were a part of that: Godsends.

There came a time when the Spirit of the Lord clearly told me that I needed to make some serious changes in my marriage. I was being asked to do some of the hardest things I had ever done. The last thing I wanted to do was cause him more pain, but I had learned that pain is purposeful. Pain propels a proliferation-like action My pain pushed me to make changes, taking me to greater places, and healthier relationships. I also knew he needed some space to explore and face the traumas from his perceptions (or misperceptions) he'd had as child, which he'd spent his whole life trying to outrun. I hoped he would stop running and face his fears, his traumas, and his shame and heal and overcome his addiction.

I have often felt very alone and invisible in my sufferings, even when surrounded by family and friends, I have come to understand that for me, loneliness is not an absence of amazing people or love. It was an absence of hope and pure faith. The Lord knew my journey was purposeful and gave me everything I needed without completely taking that valuable and purposeful pain away.

Our Savior is merciful without removing the purposeful.

You can get through your hard. Invite the Lord to be on your journey with you. He may take you places that are hard, but they will be the very purposeful hard that you need, at the time you need it, to become the you that your spirit wants and knows you to be. You can't go wrong if you walk this journey with the Lord. He will ensure that you reach your destination.

Life update

There came a time when the Spirit of the Lord clearly directed me in what to do in my marriage. I acted on that prompting and it was hard! I stopped being in charge of trying to help my husband overcome his addiction and allowed him to choose to feel his pain and face his traumas without me driving it.

As I followed the hard and sometimes very painful promptings I received, he had to step up and figure things out on his own. I was no longer there to be his crutch. He has been doing and continues to do the hard work. He has gotten clean from the drugs that had numbed him from dealing with trauma. He has been making changes and has had some very sweet experiences. I have learned in my study of Christ's life that Christ Himself had boundaries. Many times, people would try to manipulate Christ and He didn't engage in their manipulative tactics because He knew that allowing them to manipulate Him would not serve them. Likewise, we are working to have strong boundaries in place, because we both know that manipulation serves the addiction and doesn't serve either of our well-being. I have encouraged him to call me out. I try to invite new perspectives. I now can safely call him out when he starts to fall into former conversational habits and he quickly owns it. He now will stop himself in the middle of a sentence and call himself out when he recognizes that he's saying things that are manipulative or untrue. I love that we are safe to call each other out. We have both grown spiritually as a result of our imperfections and weaknesses. We are enjoying each other more than ever. The snags don't get in the way; they just offer us new insights. I realize that this is not always the outcome for those who have loved ones who suffer through addiction. But I want you to know that as the spouse of an addicted husband, you can find peace, understanding, and strength in Christ, in support groups, in understanding addiction, and in not allowing your subconscious brain to rule. I know that we would not be where we are without our Savior who so lovingly leads and lifts us. Whatever your story, I hope that you will find your support in Christ and in others who validate and lift you. This was not done to me, but for me. The pain and anguish in my struggles were necessary for the birth of a new, more emotionally resilient, perfectly imperfect me.

7

OVERCOMING
THE IMPOSSIBLE

By Amy Varney

When I was a child, or even when I was graduating high school, if anyone had told me that I would be where I am now, I would never have believed them. Let me be real. I always dreamed of having a big family and being married to my best friend, but I never imagined all the things that I would have to go through to get to that point. For years I had blocked the abuse that had happened to me when I was young and I had many life experiences that shaped me along the way. My life was like a creek or river with pebbles and stones that felt massive to work through and impossible to overcome, but I slowly found a way around or through. It was in February 2014 that some of the worst memories and experiences in my life were unlocked. Little did I know at that time that it would be three more years before an arrest would be made. During those years, I would experience emotions and crippling anxiety like I'd never known.

The little girl inside of me wanted to feel heard but was scared to death of being judged or looked down upon. She was so very vulnerable and afraid.

If I started to tell people about what had happened to me, what would they think? What would my family think? What would my kids think? I wanted to protect my kids. I wanted to protect my family. I didn't want to be *that* person; I didn't want to be "the victim." There was so much my younger self had blocked—so much! The pain of not having stopped it; had I only said something . . . so much anxiety over how to just be.

Over time, the anxiety evolved into OCD, except there was nothing compulsive about it. I had to control everything around me and make everything perfect because if everything was perfect then there would be nothing for anyone to judge. When you spend all your time and energy trying to control things that are beyond your control, you fall into a cycle of exploding when things aren't perfect, then apologizing for exploding, then becoming depressed because you feel like a failure and a terrible mother, and you find your happiness is drained from you little by little. Before you know it, you're just going through the motions and getting triggered by everything around you. I had a friend once say that if you think of yourself as being triggered by everyone around you, it's like walking around with a bunch of buttons and allowing people to push those buttons and giving them control over you. That visual forever changed the way I look at things.

February 2014

The memory that flashed into my head was like a bad dream. It took my breath away. There's no way this could be real! There's no way I would have forgotten something like this. Maybe I had seen too many CSI shows. I quickly called my counselor and begged to get in the next day and then proceeded to cry on and off for the rest of the day with the horrible images in my head. It physically triggered so much inside of me. I was in shock. I couldn't eat. I barely slept. When I did sleep, I had nightmares. I was unprepared for what was to come.

The hardest thing I did was to get out of the car and walk into the office with a huge pit of dread in my stomach and the feeling like I would throw up at any moment. Just getting from the car into the office for the appointment, I felt like I was met with every obstacle. It was like, subconsciously I didn't want to go. This happened at every appointment afterwards for a long time—it was a struggle because subconsciously, I didn't want to dig into any of it.

That's when the questions began. How old was I when the abuse was happening? Where was I (location) and where was my mom? How could this have happened? Why did this happen to me? This can't be real, can it?! It was real. It did happen. I had been drop kicked into a pit of darkness that left me feeling like a terrified little child. I felt no hope. How could I survive this? How was I supposed to still be a mom to my large family and do all that was expected of me? How were people going to react when they knew? Shame, fear, terror . . . all these feelings accompanied me daily. Behind my smile lay the darkness that no one knew I was hiding. If only they knew.

March–April 2014

As my subconscious began to release memories, it was a slow and painful download. Part of me wanted an instant download just to get it over with and the other part of me didn't want to remember anything because it was so hard. There were times that I would wake up in the middle of the night, sick from the memory of what had happened, and I would vomit all over my bed. My husband would gather all of the bedding off the bed, and then scoop me into his arms. When my reaction to his tender loving care was to push him away and try to escape his arms, telling him he didn't need to do this, that he hadn't signed up for this, his response was, "You're mine. I love you. This is not your fault." Other times I couldn't bear to be touched because of that feeling of being dirty and ruined. When I shared these feelings with my husband—that I was worthless, that I was not worthy of his love—he reassured me that there was nothing that had been done to me that would ever take his love from me.

One of the most difficult nights came when I realized that I must tell my parents. The abuse had been horrific and the family gatherings that were happening included the uncle who had abused me. It was unthinkable. How would I tell my parents? How would they react? I asked to talk with both of them in person and when I showed up without my kids in tow, to my parents' credit, they knew it was serious. I shared only a few details and swore them to secrecy. I had an urgent and crucial feeling that the details and what had happened must stay quiet (I had learned from all those crime shows and did not want anyone to warn the offender). They swore they wouldn't say anything to anyone (does that ever really work?) and I then told them about my most clear and concrete memory. I was five years old and had been in my aunt and uncle's home. I could describe the bathroom in minute detail . . .the tile, the towels, the carpet, the closet and the clothes that were hanging in the closet . . . and everything my uncle did to me when he raped me. I recalled him tossing me into the closet when my aunt walked in looking for me. I remember scrambling to hide so she wouldn't see and I wouldn't be punished (for the threats he told me kept me silent). The scene played through my head like a movie: so many terrible details. The counselor said it was a vivid recollection because my conscious mind wanted to focus on the details around me and not on what was happening to me. It was a way to protect my mind from the trauma and shock.

My parents listened and I feared my father would lose all self-control and shoot my uncle. My mother sobbed uncontrollably as she kept repeating, "how did this happen?" She truly rarely left me with anyone and it was a sucker punch of the worst kind for her to hear about this vivid nightmare of abuse.

Seeing their reaction was all the more crushing. I wanted to protect them from the darkness. I didn't want to speak it out loud. It made it too real, too terrifying.

We agreed not to speak of it until there was something else to discuss. That "something else" came all too soon.

May 2014: Meeting with the detective

Wow! The legal process is crazy specific! I could write a book about this process alone. I had interviews with the intake officer, interviews with the detective assigned the case, interviews about all the memories that had surfaced so far, and on and on. Other than reliving the memories, going through the interview with the lead detective felt like an interrogation and was one of the more diffuse things I have ever endured. There were *so* many questions and details—so specific that after several hours of questioning, my head would hurt. I felt like the detective thought I was lying. I felt like he thought I was stupid. I felt turned upside down and inside out and I never wanted to speak of the abuse again. At least he made that that part a little easier: he put me under a gag order. I wasn't to talk to anyone other than him or my counselor about any of the memories relating to the case. That was difficult on so many levels, especially because as my memories were surfacing, so were my cousins' memories. And the investigation began.

Summer 2014

It's hard to try and heal and claw your way up and out of the well of darkness when you have six sweet children at home all summer. I was exhausted and drained. I had little to no patience. I knew I had to change. I went to counseling every week. I applied every technique I could to release the anger, hurt, fear, repulsion, confusion, and overwhelm, and I began noticing a difference. I realized my need for perfection and control came from being controlled by an abuser when I was a child. That truth and knowledge was profound. Anytime I found myself getting angry or acting out of my need to control, I would stop and recognize that this was a result of my experiences from my uncle's behavior. I didn't want to control my children—I am *not* my uncle! This first breakthrough helped me to create a barrier that began to feel protective for my family and me. I remember the first time I recognized that I was acting on this breakthrough and seeing the effects that my control had had upon my children. One of my children had broken something and his look told me that he expected me to explode with anger. But my first reaction was to not care about what had been broken and instead say to my child, "How can I help you? Are you ok?" His shocked look helped me to see that *this* is how I want to parent. I told him that things can be replaced but *he* could not be replaced, that accidents and mistakes happen, that I wanted him to be a kid and that I did not want to get angry anymore. This was progress in my healing.

I wish that was all that it would take to keep the darkness at bay, but the darkness comes and seeps into every bit of happiness when you least expect it. Feelings of self-doubt and unworthiness to be loved hung on everything I said and did and threatened to ruin every good memory I made. There were times when I didn't want to live. It was just too painful. It was just too hard to face everything. I just wanted the hurt and the pain and the shame to go away. Everyone would be hurt if I ceased to live, but they would be much better off without me. I was angry. Angry at God for not stopping this. Angry at the adults in my life for not protecting me. Angry that I was adopted and had to endure this abuse. Angry at everyone I could find to be angry at (but I wasn't angry at my kids so much anymore). I didn't want to even go to church because I was worried something would happen to my kids or someone would find out and talk bad about me and judge me. It was a vicious cycle.

One night my cousin reached out and invited me over. There were a few of us there and we had all gone and talked with the detective. We kept our confidences and didn't talk details. We mainly shared our feelings: shame, fear, guilt at what we were putting our families through, anger, and, highest on the list, the darkness that threatened that we would be better off ceasing to exist. A lot of tears were shed. A lot of hugs were given. The biggest blessing of the evening was knowing I wasn't alone. My cousins were suffering everything I was. Every emotion! I knew I could reach out to them and they would understand. Even when it was a simple text of "today sucks" or "uncle (insert name here) sucks." I wasn't alone. This wasn't my fault. I will survive this. Some days I would repeat this five times before I could even get out of bed.

October–November 2014

One clear memory came on a night around the time of my birthday and I remember sobbing and asking my husband for a divorce because he didn't sign up for this and he couldn't possibly love me through this darkness and devastation. As I ugly cried with tears and snot running down my face, he looked me straight in the eye and said, "I'm not going anywhere and YOU didn't ask for this and it isn't your fault or who you are. I fell in love with the woman you ARE. The experiences you have gone through have made you WHO you are and who I love. I'm in this forever." I clung to him in desperation, both to feel safe and secure and to know he was real and not a dream. I didn't feel worthy of his love and this would play a huge part in my recovery, though at the time but I didn't know those feelings of being unworthy of love would be so impactful.

February 2015

My father died unexpectedly. He had a stroke and was gone six days later. My biggest supporter and #1 fan was gone. How was I going to get through this?

In that same month a warrant was issued for my uncle's arrest. More legal stuff followed and I was so thankful I wasn't alone. I hated what we were going through. I hated feeling like the victim (even though that _100_ % was what I was). I hated everything that had happened. There was a LOT of hate in me. Every counseling session helped relieve it but it clung to everything and finding joy was so hard when I felt like I was suffocating.

We had a beautiful funeral for my dad and I felt so thankful that there was a tangible strength that ran through our family in our grief—love and memories of him—uniting us.

One of the difficult things was that whenever I was extremely emotional, I would turn to food as a comfort and coping mechanism and as such, I was the largest I had ever been not being pregnant. I feel like it was almost my way of trying to make myself unattractive because I didn't feel worthy to be loved. Everything came to a head when I saw a picture of myself with some of my music students and I realized how unhappy I was with myself physically (not just mentally) and I knew something had to change and it had to change quickly. I am blessed to have a sister-in-law I could call to ask advice and get answers from. I signed up for classes and began exercising steadily for the first time (really) in my life (other than when I was a young girl and teenager). Mentally, my workouts pushed me past the boundaries of what I physically thought I was capable of and I started to lift out of the darkness faster and more easily than I had with just counseling alone. I realized that our hormones and emotions are directly tied to each other and as I exercised, my hormones and emotions began leveling out. I started to be the fun mom that I had previously been and I didn't feel suffocated or drowned in the darkness of it all. We had to endure some hard things with my uncle being in jail and standing before the judge to tell him why bail should not be granted; it made me want to throw up and at the same time curl in a ball and suck my thumb and cry my eyes out. None of us knew that the trial would take almost four years before it was finished. During those years, I relied foremost on my husband and also my support system for strength. I had let them see me at my most vulnerable and they loved me through it all anyway. I knew that as much as I hated this process, I wasn't alone and if nothing else, I knew I had said something and hopefully protected others from being abused.

Fall 2015

Oh, how the healing comes in waves! I had to break through not feeling worthy to love myself because I was so damaged and dark from the abuse I had endured. I had been angry at God and not allowing His light into my life. I worked with my counselor to learn to allow myself to feel love. When I finally got to that space, I was on a high and it was one of the happiest times for our family. The saying "when momma is happy everyone's happy" = truth! I engaged in daily prayers, exercising, weekly counseling, lots of family activities and outside time. I felt safe, loved, secure and I no longer felt like a victim. I felt empowered and courageous.

On Christmas in 2015 we found out we were expecting baby number seven. We were thrilled! We told the kids at Disneyland! In February of 2016, I had still continued to exercise and eat healthy; allowing myself a reward meal or treat once a week (because anything more would make me fall off the wagon, so to speak) helped, too. My mindset was key and I allowed myself to feel, really *feel,* my emotions instead of stuffing them away and hiding them. I had learned to recognize that the more I validated my own emotions, the easier it was to move through them and work with them instead of ignoring them and fighting against them. I recognized when I needed help and instead of thinking that I could do everything on my own (really, can any of us ever do it all on our own?) I would think, No! And I would reach out for help.

Fall of 2016

I gave birth to our beautiful baby girl and our family was on a high. Heaven's blessings and healing on every level. We had some beautiful memories made and those helped us through three miscarriages until I was able to sustain being pregnant with our caboose and baby #8 who was due to come spring of 2019.

Fall 2018

I had no idea how hard it was going to be to revisit everything but in the fall of 2018, reliving it became real. Trial was set for September but then was delayed for the New Year. Pregnant with our last child and unsure of how things would unfold, I tried to prepare for it the best I could. Fortunately, I was still having regular counseling sessions and had made changes in my life to allow for me to take care of me: meditation, eating healthy, and exercising, to name a few.

My cousin began teaching a beautiful program about emotional resilience and I jumped in head first, excited for her inspiration and the prospect of more tools to help me in being free of the pain and finding joy in life. The most impactful life lesson I learned in The Dig is that my limiting beliefs are not real. The *feel* very real, but they aren't actually real. As we release those limiting beliefs—as we release the *weight* of those beliefs—and we release the judgments we experience from those beliefs, we open ourselves up to feeling love.

This is a life-changing principle for me.

Message of hope

Do you remember how I mentioned reaching out for help? Over the years, I have gathered amazing tools to use! I also talked with friends that I trusted and confided in and I didn't keep my fears, discouragement, depression, anxiety, and self-judgements in the dark. If you are in that dark place, reach up. I know how that dark place feels. I know what it's like to feel alone, like nobody is there, nobody loves you, nobody could possibly understand or relate to you or even want to love you because of the dark things that have happened to you. I know that place and I want you to know that you are not alone. Someone else has been there and climbed out of that dark hole and wants to help you out. I know that the process of climbing out of that hole, of dealing with everything that put you there, is almost as much hell as everything that happened to put you into that darkness. But I am here, with my hand out, to help pull you up out of that dark hole and into the light. The darkness hates the light, loves secrets, and hates truth! The healing journey that brings you out of the darkness can be frustrating. But keep going. You will find that on your journey, you will meet others on the same kind of journey.

I have come to realize that I am drawn to people (or people are drawn to me) who have experienced abuse and trauma. We have met in ways and places that had nothing to do with "healing" or abuse or trauma. I had one experience of meeting a woman in an online club we had both joined and we decided to meet for lunch. During lunch, the woman just started sharing her story, which inspired me to share my story. As we concluded our lunch, she told me that I radiate light, and that she wants to radiate light for others.

I know that facing the memories and the darkness can be scary. But as I have healed, I have realized that I am not those things that took me into the dark. Those who did hurtful things to me are the dark. I am light. As you heal, please know that the darkness that you feel is *not* you. That darkness is from those who hurt you. You have light in you. Feel the light you have in yourself. Allow that light to heal you.

8

GOODBYE "YES GIRL"

By Sherri Stradling

As a mother and now a grandma, I know what it's like to desire all the wisdom of the ages and God's direction to guide my path with the family He has blessed me with. But desire alone, or even countless hours of studying, won't guarantee a clear path illuminated perfectly with light and truth. Desire does, however, grant a person the next, best step for them to take with the knowledge and experience they have accumulated so far on their path. Some call this "learning line-upon-line." Since the days of learning that knowledge is power, I have prayed for the power of discernment in seeking truth. Through the years, I have learned that not everything in books (and especially on the internet) is correct just because it's in print, or someone with credentials (like Dr. Spock) says so.

I believe my mother truly thought she was doing right— encouraging me and perhaps trying to build my self-esteem—when she asked me to do a task that she probably could have done herself. It was a simple task that only required me to return a glass casserole dish to our neighbor. I was only four-years old, but I remember it like it was yesterday, maybe because it was the first time in my life I was old enough to actually help my mom and feel valued in her praise. She told me that I could do this task because I wasn't shy like her, but outgoing like my dad. Despite all the fear pounding in my tiny heart, her words (and probably some adrenaline flowing through my veins!) propelled me outward after she opened the door of our blue, two-door, Plymouth sedan, then lifted the lever that would allow me to climb out from the back seat. Little did I know, I was climbing out of the shadows and into the light of false pride. That moment would also mark the beginning of a new me: a new, confident, uninhibited, outgoing, four-year-old *false* me.

Yes, that day I learned how to shut out the fearful chatter in my head and the signs of anxiety in my body. I got out of the car and carried the dish, rang the doorbell, and went on to have a very adult conversation with the neighbor, thanking her and offering information about how well my mom and my new baby sister were doing. We then said our goodbyes and she closed her house door. As that door closed, I also closed the door to the "old" (though very young) me, and I walked back to the car, to my mom, with my shoulders back and head held high . . . a new, proud, *yes girl!*

Just three months later I started kindergarten, where this new confidence came in handy because I had to ride the 'big kids' bus to school, with kids in all the grades from kindergarten to twelfth grade. I've never been able to recall in which month of that year the following trauma occurred. For many of my adult years, I couldn't even label the event as "traumatic" because I thought a person had to physically hurt another person in order to cause actual trauma. It must have been early in the school year because I wasn't wearing a coat or long pants. I had on one of my new, beautiful, homemade skirt outfits, which granted easy access to my body under my clothes if a boy wanted that access . . . and on this particularly dark day, one boy did.

I remember making the great effort to climb up the big steps onto the bus, only to find all the seats were taken. I fearfully made my way down the length of the bus, though I was already in the full mode of using my new skills to ignore my fears and pretend I wasn't scared. I'm certain my eyes gave me away, though, as I silently pleaded to each onlooker to let me sit with them. Finally, I made eye contact with a boy who motioned for me to come sit on his lap, patting his thigh as if I were a puppy who should just be grateful for his generosity. And I was grateful! I can never forget the distinct relief I felt to be welcomed to sit with him, and then the paralysis of mind and body I experienced from his unwelcome touch. By the time the bus arrived at the school, I was relieved to finally get away from his unwelcome touch.

This boy, my hero, the one who came to my rescue, also stole my innocence (right in public) as he touched me inappropriately. All that was stuck in my head about his actions was that I was the bad one because I did nothing about it. For years I could never understand how I just sat there without saying a word. As a result of this experience, from that time forward, I believed that I was a bad girl and, having already created a false 'yes girl,' I was easily able to hide what had happened to me and *do* everything I could to *be* a good girl, further cementing my false 'yes girl' identity.

For just under a quarter of a century, I didn't dare tell my parents or any other adult this awful secret. It wasn't until something similar happened to a precious little girl, also only the age of a kindergartner, that I realized my own innocence on that bus that day nearly twenty-five years before. Since that little girl wasn't a bad girl, I must not have been a bad girl. Sadly, seeing the truth for her didn't make it magically, completely true for me. I learned that changing that limiting belief of myself would not fully happen for another quarter of a century, but that little girl's experience did finally help me break my own silence.

I told the little girl's mom about the boy on the bus, then pleaded with this mother to make sure her daughter *knew* she wasn't a bad girl so that she wouldn't spend all of the beginning years of life thinking something was wrong with her; that she was bad and in some way asked for it; or worst of all, that she somehow deserved it (as I had thought I did). You see, because I believed that all those years ago I was a bad girl and because I had carried that secret of what had happened on the bus, I developed a deep desire to be labeled a "good girl." This desire took root in my child heart and I did everything I was told to do, and then some. I developed a need to be praised and the higher the ranking of authority a person had over me, the greater I worked to earn their high esteem of me. As the oldest child in my family, I had many opportunities to help, so I became the "best little helper" I could be—not just at home, but everywhere.

As an adult I would continue these actions, which included countless times of saying 'yes' when someone needed me; 'yes' even if I didn't want to; 'yes' because it was the right thing to do; 'yes' when it wasn't convenient or even possible; 'yes' at the detriment of my current limitations, personal needs, or needs of those close to me. Don't get me wrong! Some of those yes answers were with a pure intent or motive. Some of those yes answers didn't interfere with anything. And some of those yes answers were sacrifices I *chose* for the better good and they are yes answers I will never regret. But many of those yes answers were said while the noise in my head was screaming NO!

I had learned to silence the trembling in my body, to turn down the volume of my feelings and meet the needs of others. While these actions of the 'yes girl,' trying to prove she was a good girl, brought into my life many friends and led to creating many cherished memories with people I will love forever (moments I am, to this day, thankful I was a part of), I am sad that I did not learn sooner to honor the 'no' that is equally a righteous, sometimes vitally necessary answer.

Thankfully, through working with some good therapists through the years, I have worked out many issues, but deep inside I could not let go of the belief that I really *was* a bad girl, and if I ever acted out on bad girl thoughts . . . That belief continued to grow stronger. I spent many years fixated on wanting to change the narrative, because if I could that, I could also take back my life: take back my God-given right to choose. I could finally LET GO of the "reality" that I had accepted for my existence in life: that since I was a bad girl, I had to *act* like I was a good girl—a 'yes girl'—which meant I *had* to help others with their needs and forget about my own needs.

There is no doubt that being a people pleaser is exhausting, but regardless (and sadly), my 'yes girl' mentality thrived on the praise from others in my need to be known as a good girl. The kudos satisfied and fueled my need to feel important. Interestingly enough, 'words of affirmation' is one of my primary love languages, so each positive word said to me made me feel loved, good enough, and valued. I deeply desired all these feelings of worth from others because deep inside, I truly believed I still was a bad girl.

Because I had learned the true joy that comes from serving others and from making good choices with a pure intent, trying to change the narrative became a particularly difficult process.

At a certain point in my life, Jesus became my everything. He spent His entire life in the service of others and because I wanted to be like Him, it became natural to me to try to live my life in the same way; why would I want to snuff that out of me? Why would I want to listen to my own needs? Wasn't this the epitome of selfishness? of being a bad girl? To say the least, coming to terms with these two opposite trains of thought was excruciating. Sometimes it still brings me to my knees in pleas to my Heavenly Father for clarity, understanding, and discernment. Clearly, there is a fine line between wanting to serve others and listening to my own needs. It often felt like I was walking on a tight rope at least until that moment in time, when in desperation, I pleaded for greater light and truth.

I was suffocating, not only in my struggle to walk this figurative tight rope, but with a choice I had made to break free from the prison I had created for myself around important relationships in my life. The courage and power it took to ultimately say *no* (for once in my life, when it really mattered) didn't come easily, but I am a witness to the reality that it did come. As a result, the great knowledge I received—of vulnerably stepping into the unknown without a plan, without even a glimpse of my future—came specifically when I found the tools from The Dig and I began working the process. Where before I had felt trapped and wanted to get out, I had gained freedom from working the process from The Dig. I felt I could do and be whatever I wanted. It all came together as a type of perfect storm to bring about the growth I had intently prayed for over so many years.

Growing pains are real and I had embarked on a journey of love and true pain. I had tricked myself into believing I had found the love of my life. He said all the right things, connected all the right dots, and offered all the right opportunities that I had missed for years. I had never before taken a chance on me, had never bet on me, and I truly believed that in breaking out of the box I had kept myself a prisoner in, I would find happiness—and I did find fleeting moments of happiness, but ultimately not joy. This relationship fell apart as quickly as it came together. Had it not been for The Dig and my Savior, I never would have recognized what did not work between us and I never could have pulled away. The day I stood my ground and stood up for what I knew was right for my family and me, was the day true confidence manifested in my life. From that day forward I have had the freedom to choose what the right, next step is for me (and not from a good girl—yes girl mentality.)

106

I love that I know to stop 'should-ing' on myself and others. I love the opportunity I have each day to wake up and choose.

It is my understanding that we often fail forward. How else would we have the invention of the light bulb? It took Thomas Edison thousands of failed attempts before he was successful. My life's experiences would suggest I am a pro at failing forward, but I don't beat myself up over it anymore. I don't see myself as a bad girl. I don't allow that limiting belief to hold me back. I choose to see myself as a spiritual being having a human experience and that often means I choose to also see myself as a "successful failure"— a concept I was introduced to over twenty-five years ago during my first failed marriage. Back then, I was taught that we are all failures; we all make choices that put us in a circular motion either spiraling forward or backward as we experience the ups and downs from those choices. Whether we are successful or unsuccessful failures all depends on who or what we turn to as a source of power when we are bouncing along the bottom. Do we unplug from that source of power (hide, lie, or isolate in shame) or do we plug into that source of power (share truth, surround ourselves with people we love, and seek help)?

I am grateful my source of power is my Savior, Jesus Christ and like an outlet, when I plug in . . . my lamp turns on and His light illuminates my path. I am grateful that lighted path led me to find tools in The Dig Method, to let go of the limiting belief that I was bad, and started me on the necessary transformative path from being the 'yes girl' to being a woman who lives life on purpose, without shame, and can better serve with a true and honest heart.

Unbreakable

9

LESSONS FROM THE WALL

By Mary Kelly

A s early as she could remember, the girl felt part of the wall. She was always standing by a wall, and somehow, the wall swallowed her up and she was just one brick of that wall. It wasn't a beautiful wall. Oh no, it was an ugly wall and one that a passerby would never notice. Feeling alone, disconnected, unseen, and unheard is probably one of the worst traumas anyone can experience.

She couldn't remember ever feeling heard. If she did speak, she instantly experienced regret. Did they stare because they thought she didn't have a tongue? Or perhaps they thought she didn't know how to speak English? She had so many memories that validated her fear of opening her mouth.

One memory from fourth grade came to mind. The girl was busy working on a project. The teacher asked where Jill was. Jill sat right next to her and she knew Jill had gone to use the restroom. She blurted out the sentence, "Jill went to the restroom." The room became silent. Every eye was on her and she wondered why the silence seemed to scream in her ears. Who was she to answer a question? Who was she to think the teacher would believe her? You are so dumb to speak up! Why did you do that? You certainly don't matter! Those words rang loudly in her brain and her heart! Those sentences were on repeat, playing over and over in her mind.

They even tested her at school once to see if she had hearing loss. She didn't. It was just the loud blaring noise of the drum of self-doubt beating so loud in her head. The noise of the badgering fear going on inside her mind drowned out the teacher's instruction, and all else for that matter.

She didn't realize it at the time, but she was being fed lies of destruction. Lies concerning our personal worth as a child of God are devastating. Negative self-talk wrapped up within the cells of our brains quickly locks us up into an isolated prison of anger and discontent. Negative self-talk is a road to hell.

The girl had no idea that her amazing, powerful, wonderful Father in Heaven was her Father. She had no idea she was made in His image. She had no idea she had a Heavenly Mother who stood as a Queen, cheering her on. She had the potential for Her qualities of beauty, mercy, intelligence, wisdom, and articulateness deep inside her, but would they ever come to bear fruit? She had heard she was a child of God. Somehow, she never really believed it. The drum of the constant beat of lies never allowed this truth to sink into her heart and mind. She believed that God loved all of His children—all except her. She believed she wasn't up to par with everyone else, that she didn't "fit the mold" of a person God could love. The girl believed that her limitations and weaknesses meant that anything she said was insignificant, dumb, and awkward. In every social setting, she wanted to bury herself deep into the wall. To this day, her self-doubt and fear trigger those beliefs. If all the attention is on her, she hears that voice inside, taunting, "What an idiot! Why did you say that? No one wanted to listen to you."

When did these feelings of isolation and disconnection begin? Did it start on December 23, 1942, when a blanket of snow filled the air? There was music playing in the LDS Hospital. It was the booming voice of Jessie Evans Smith singing "He that Hath Clean Hands and a Pure Heart." She probably remembered it because her mother told her about the difficult birth and the beautiful, booming voice of Jessie Evans Smith. However, the images she had in her mind from what her mother described from her birth made her feel that she somehow could remember the empty, white, sterile walls of the hospital, and every time she heard that song, something within her stirred. A memory of some sort, calling to her. Was it saying to her that she wasn't really alone? Was it saying, "It is okay to speak up"? Or did the song simply invoke homesickness that would last her entire life—a homesickness for the heavenly home she had left behind when she came into this world in that sterile room with its confining walls?

She knew something was missing. She knew something was wrong. She could feel it deep within the pit of her stomach. The constant heckling of her mind saying, "You goober! You idiot! Why did you speak? Who do you think you are?" The feeling of isolation often caused her to be sick. She was poor—really poor. She moved from place to place with no lasting friendships. The pain in her gut, the sickness she experienced in her body, was ever-present. She had to eat, but everything she ate made her sick. There was no money for doctors, but back then, doctors probably wouldn't have known the cause anyway.

It wasn't until she was thirty-four years old that she would learn that the cause of her poor gut health was an auto-immune disorder—celiac sprue. She had suffered from it all of her life. For all those years, she had struggled with constant physical problems, feeling like nobody would understand her frequent trips to the restroom, constant fatigue, lack of energy and strength, and the pain throughout her body. Receiving the diagnosis for the cause of her physical suffering and learning how to monitor the disease was helpful, but so much damage had already been done.

She had not grown. She had not absorbed vitamins from her food. From the age of sixteen, she'd had pain that kept her from really having fun or enjoying any activity. The pain was rarely quiet. Everything was harder for her. Nothing came easy. School was hard. Creativity was very difficult. Relationships were so hard and usually not joyful. She grew up mostly among adults, so she didn't participate often in the activities that most children participated in, such as biking or swimming or games.

She could not hear love. She had a good mother and father. They did love her, but she just could not hear it somehow. She could not feel love. She could not speak love. Love was locked up inside her. Something was blocking the reception. Something was blocking the redemption. She devalued anyone's opinion who said she was loved, pretty, or of worth. She simply looked at them in disgust and thought they were crazy. They just were not in touch with reality. They simply did not know what they were talking about. She judged their intentions. She felt cut off from them. She thought they were imposters in the most distasteful of ways.

She did not trust girls. In fact, she disliked most girls. She disliked being in meetings with just girls or women. Girls gossiped and they were critical. They judged her every move. Their judgments were not laced with mercy. She was always the last one chosen. She was always the one that no one really wanted to be friends with at school. She rarely smiled. She stood on the sidelines and watched all the laughter, feeling numb on the inside. She felt she could never be like the girl in the group who was happy, always smiling and having fun. She could not understand how that happy girl got people to respond to her the way they did, to connect with the happy girl. No, this girl felt frozen, still, cold, isolated, disconnected, unimportant, fearful, and alone. Who was she? She was no one!

She had no talents or gifts to share or give. Once, an insightful male teacher seemed to know she needed to shine. He asked her to bring something to school that she had created. She couldn't think of anything. However, she had planted sunflowers with her mom. They had grown into gigantic beautiful flowers. She loved how they followed the sun. She loved the brilliant yellow petals and the dark brown centers. She loved how they hung heavy on the stem as if they were almost too good for the ugly field they grew in. She took some sunflowers to school and the teacher was so nice. Unlike the female teachers the girl had such negative experiences with, this male teacher was trying to give her a chance to have a voice. For the first time, the girl thought she might have a talent for speaking, but she and her family soon moved away and the girl once again had no voice to speak, no ears to hear.

This prison of self-loathing and discontent was dark. She considered suicide. She thought of running away. She thought there was no way out. College didn't change the situation; counseling didn't free her from her prison; and marriage and children were not the magic cure. She could not feel a connection with a mother, a father, a friend, a husband, or even with a child. How could she ever feel it with God? Even when she was seeing a counselor, taking prescription medications, trying health food remedies, and living the commandments, she still experienced the ache of loneliness, still felt the sharp edges of rejection and failure. She still could not find her voice or feel any comfort. Children born, children cherished, children loved deeply, children prayed for, children prioritized—but as a young mother, she was so overwhelmed trying to help her children to be happy and productive while also trying to keep up with the dishes and laundry and other necessary household chores, that she experienced lonely days and nights.

So, what *did* free the girl from the bonds of self-doubt, fear, and low self-esteem? There was a light. Here is the story of the dispensation of light that came into her life over the years, gradually, like the dawn that slowly breaks over the hills and fields and mountains and waves. It came. It came in the name of grace.

The first glimmer of light was a job. With earnings from her job, she saved money for a new dress and a new purse. She absolutely loved them. The dress was rustic red and not just any kind of dress. It was the perfect dress—one she would never forget. The purse was green—not just any green purse, but the perfect color of green and the perfect style. She paid tithing on the money she'd made from her job. She paid it, not because she was good, but because something inside her said it was very important for her to obey this commandment. She did, and miracles happened. She never applied for a scholarship. However, the morning of her high school graduation ceremonies, she felt something new and good— a sort of anticipation of happiness. During the ceremonies, they announced her name as winning a scholarship to Brigham Young University in Provo, Utah. It was the beginning of a series of miracles. It was also the beginning of long years of hard work, sacrifice, and a lack of fun and games.

The miracles kept rolling in. While she was in college, she would often stumble over a box of food left on her doorstep. She would find envelopes of money stuffed in her college books. She would fail a class and take it over again. She would fall asleep from lack of food and sleep. Assignments did not come easily. Understanding new ideas was difficult. She would look around at those having fun and beg Heavenly Father for happiness. "What are they so happy about?" she would ask. She never did find the source of their happiness. There was no pot of gold at the end of the rainbow. But happiness began to be an option. It began to be a choice. After eight years of blood, sweat, and tears, she graduated from college.

The girl read two books in college that greatly influenced her. The first one was *Man's Search for Meaning: An Introduction to Logotherapy* by Viktor E. Frankl. She had no understanding of the word "logotherapy." The book, though—the written words from Viktor E. Frankl's book spoke to her very soul! She had a choice! Victor Frankl had written: "Everything can be taken from a man but one thing: the last of human freedoms—to choose one's attitude in any given set of circumstances, to choose one's own way . . . Between stimulus and response there is a space. In that space is our power to choose our response. In our response lies our growth and our freedom."

She knew this message about choosing one's attitude and responses to circumstances was important! She knew that she needed to incorporate these choices into her life. Doing so was the battle of a lifetime—a battle still raging at times. But it is a battle better won after many years of struggle.

This new knowledge that she had a choice in how she would react to all she would experience was precious. It was a treasure! She remembered being rejected by someone she thought loved her. It was a trial, but not just any trial. It was another validation that she was not enough. She wasn't valued or treasured. She was just left by the wall again. But the book! The book kept repeating over and over in her mind, "You have a choice." The choice became loud and clear. It said simply—move forward. You have agency. You are responsible for who you are. The choice was to silence the aching heart and move forward. She knew she had a choice. She did not have to be a victim, disappearing into the wall just because the one she deeply loved didn't love her. She had a choice. She could choose.

The second book that influenced and shaped her way out of her self-doubt prison was The Book of Mormon. The escape from that prison did not come easily. It came with prayer. It came with fasting.

It came through intense study. The study was consistent over many years. She knew God lived. She knew Jesus Christ was real. As she studied this Book of Mormon that she held in her hands, she came to recognize the power in that book. She could hear the power rustling through the pages. She could feel its power from under her pillow where she had put the book the night before. She could hear the power of its music as she clutched it to her chest and danced around the room. She had come to know her Savior within those rustling pages day in and day out, word upon word, line upon line, pondering upon pondering, year after year. She learned lessons that she could apply in her real life. The lessons she learned from the Book of Mormon were written upon her heart!

The first lesson she learned was to hold on and not give up. Hold on because, as is recorded in the Book of Mormon in 1 Nephi 16:29, "by small means, the Lord can bring about great things!" This message is punctuated later in the Book of Mormon in Alma 37:6: "that by small and simple things are great things brought to pass; and small means in many instances doth confound the wise." She read these verses at a time when she needed this message. Her husband was on call at the hospital that week and for several days she had been home alone with her two little boys. She was pregnant with her third child and she didn't feel well. She felt overwhelmed. The message, "by small and simple things are great things brought to pass" came to mind. She believed those words. She wanted to get out of the house. She wanted to stop the haunting feelings of gloom. She wanted to run a marathon. So, she strapped the baby to her pregnant body and pushed the toddler in the stroller around the block. That was the beginning. It began literally with small and simple steps. She did run marathons. Marathons fed her soul. She loved running and feeling the freedom beneath her feet. She loved how it made her mind feel. It was a habit that she would love and a habit that would sustain her through the years.

Emotional resilience is also really strengthened by small and simple habits. These habits, continued over time, increase power. She had found in her life that by small and simple choices in her habits, she could meet her challenges (challenges that are still constantly before her each day). These habits consist of prayer, meditation, scripture study, listening to or reading words of influential righteous people, choosing to think optimistic thoughts, and repeating mantras to herself. It dawned on her that what she ate, how she exercised, and the thoughts she focused on had a great impact on the quality of her life.

This helped her to see the importance of compound interest. She knew she could save small amounts of money consistently and with intention, and over time, her investment would earn interest and eventually, that earned interest could sustain her. By small and simple things, miracles can grow in the same way. She began to see that wise money habits and wise food choices would nourish rather than deplete; wise habits of exercise would build strength; and wise emotional and spiritual choices would impact her by building interest and improving the quality of her life.

Recently, she experienced something that made her want to shrink back into the wall. She felt very dumb in a group of women. The desire to retreat or run away and never return reared its ugly head again. She had been taught from Mosiah 4:30 that she needed to watch her thoughts, words, and deeds in order to experience the peace of God. She had been taught by a good friend and counselor that there is always a Guide within us and also a Goober within us, and each was striving for her attention. She remembered in this instance to sort out the talk between the Guide and the Goober. The Guide was the Spirit of the Lord who spoke the truth. He would speak to her about the truth of the past, the truth of the present, and the truth of the future. The Goober within her would speak words of defeat and beat the drum of retreat. He would want her to beat herself up over every word she spoke and over every effort she made to connect to others.

When this recent trigger came up, she repeated in her mind the following: "You made an honest mistake. The mistake does not identify you. Mistakes can be corrected and they can be forgotten and forgiven. You are deeply loved by God. You are forgiven by God, and you are a new creature in Jesus Christ. God knows who you are and He knows what He thinks of you and it is good!" The Goober began chanting, "Yeah, but you are so dumb! You will never be able to get it. You just are a jerk among people. You are just not enough among women. You are just not enough. Remember, you are the one that fades into the wall! You don't deserve to be heard. No one wants to hear you. No one wants to see you. Who do you think you are? Dumb, dumb, dumb." The sound was brassy in her ears and it began to make her head hurt. She had to confront the Goober. She had to turn it around. So, she said, "Yeah, but God! But God!" That was the message she gave the Goober.

God could and would turn it around for her. God was bigger than that Goober. God was bigger than her problems. Jesus came to earth and suffered and died for her. He came for the poor man as well as for the rich man. He came for the C student as well as for the A student. He came for the unpopular person as well as the sought-after person. He came for the person who cleans the church building as well as for the prophet. He came for the sinner and for the saint. He came for the girl beside the wall. He came to help in time of need. He came to enable us all to change, to grow, and to become.

Oh, His grace! His grace to save and to enable drowns out the Goober's voice! The Goober's voice only has power for a short time. The girl knows things will happen that encourage her to fall back into the victim mode—to that wall that is so very comfortable. She knows she will be tempted to shrink back into the wall and stay there forever. However, with the small and simple habits she has formed, she now can more easily recognize what is happening and pull herself out of the wall more quickly and effectively each time. These small and simple steps really did work magic in her life. However, like most wonderful treasures, these small and simple habits must be protected throughout time, and that protection comes through continual practice and recognizing the power of this treasure.

Some of the practices she has learned from the Dig Model have led her to incorporate the small and simple habits of prayer, scripture study, meditation, and repeating mantras. The Dig taught her to ask questions about how she *feels* about an event and whether those feelings about an event cause her to fight or freeze; assess whether her thoughts are true and even if her thoughts are true, to evaluate if those thoughts serving her; if her thoughts aren't serving her, determine what can she change about the thought; and when she changes a thought, discover how that new thought makes her feel? She has learned the small and simple habit of trying to reach out and serve someone in some small way every day, which has helped her to forget herself. She learned good habits of eating and exercising and knew they impacted her power to sort out the voices of the Guide and the Goober.

Before learning to incorporate small and simple habits into her life, she felt like she was encapsulated in a bubble that kept her from connecting with God and with others. As she has come to recognize that God has a plan for her life, that she has agency—a choice that makes her responsible for what she thinks, what she creates, what small and simple habits she engages in—she has learned that she is a child of God. She has come to recognize that she has a divine birthright that makes her as valuable as any other person on earth. She has come to recognize that her body is a temple and that she is 100% responsible for making sure that her small and simple habits will bring to pass great and wonderful outcomes. Choice, agency, and accountability all work in her life for her good. Before these realizations, she had somehow not learned the power of choice and accountability by observation. This revelation for her had come through her study of the written word of God and then her courage to keep up the habits of small and simple things.

From her study of The Book of Mormon, she also learned to remember! There are so many scriptures in the Book of Mormon that taught her about remembering. Her favorite, Helaman 5:12, teaches, "remember, remember that it is upon the rock of our Redeemer, who is Christ, the Son of God, that you must build your foundation." Then, when problems come and challenges hit you hard, when you are brought to your knees and you see no way out of misery, because of the rock upon which you have built your life— the rock which is a sure foundation—you will be able to stand and you will be able to move forward. Remember, help is coming. There is deliverance and there is a Deliverer. Remember who you are and where you have come from. Remember your divine birthright!

She was reminded from 1 Nephi 11:17 that God loves His children. She often needed to remember that she was a child of God. She had his DNA, so to speak, inside her very person. Most of all, despite all the errors she had made, all the terrible mistakes, and despite the horrors of this world, God *does* love His children. He loves her! He loves those around her. Today, when she is tempted to look at others and compare herself to them and to think, "I don't have these talents. I don't have those leadership abilities. I don't have that beauty or that money," she remembers that she has a divine birthright that makes her as valuable as anyone else on earth. That divine birthright makes her valuable just because she exists. She also remembers that there is a bigger picture playing out that we can't see or comprehend yet, and that remembrance has helped her breathe and relax more.

Although sadness, guilt, pain, grief, disappointment, failures, and sins are all experiences in life, she has learned that they don't constitute who she is and they are not meant to be the substance of her life. She learned from 2 Nephi 2:25 that "Adam fell that men might be and men are that they might have joy." Remember, all things work together to help us achieve that joy! It might take time and pondering and waiting, and to some degree, handing our power over to God, but joy is always coming.

Years ago, she read a book by George MacDonald titled *Phantastes*. In this book, she fell in love with goodness. Goodness holds magic for her. It is sweet to her soul. The opposition that rears its ugly head over and over in her mind and soul is real and she still encounters it often. She is by no means perfect—in fact, she feels far from it. She falls down all the time and doesn't act like she wants to. She *wants* to reflect the Savior and bring others to Him. But she continues to fail. The lesson she has learned, however, is not to let the failures and the falls *keep* her down. She is much better at getting up and trying again and not caring what others may or may not think of her. She loves goodness more, especially as she ages. There is something from that land of righteousness that blows sweetly in her hair and upon her cheek and she knows it is the thing that brings peace and love to her. It is the only song that sings to her heart. That peace that comes from seeking for and remembering all that is good and beautiful brings unspeakable delight and joy to her and she knows she doesn't want to partake of anything that would lead her away from that peace.

At the end of *Phantastes*, the hero was told by the guide, "A great good is coming—is coming—is coming to you!" And the hero believed it. He said, "Yet I know that good is coming to me—that good is always coming, though few have at all times the simplicity and the courage to believe it."

So, the girl tries to remember—good is coming! The fact that all things work together for her good is written on the fleshy tablets of her heart. She remembers to cultivate the faith and the courage to move forward. The road is never easy for her. She remembers that she must be aware of what enters her brain. Music, TV, social media, movies, books, and people all influence her brain and spirit. This message from the Book of Mormon has served her well. She remembers to dig herself out of self-pity. She remembers to try hard not to play the victim role. She remembers to keep going. Just keep moving and believe good is always coming. On the hard days and on the good days, she remembers she has a Deliverer and He is Jesus Christ. He is her Savior. He is her friend. He is her advocate. Above all else, she knows how critical it is to have meaningful encounters with the Lord. She knows it is the thing that has saved her. She remembers that He has redeemed her with His amazing grace. She will be not only saved from sin and death, but she also will be saved from herself! That has been a great guiding light that reminds her to not give up.

It is not over until it is over, she tells herself. She came to this earth with DNA passed down through her mother and her father and generations before them. Experiences with the Savior have determined her ability to keep getting up. Once, when she visited Jerusalem, she strayed from the tour and sat all alone on the hill overlooking the city of Jerusalem. She was tired of herself. She had failed again. Anger had once again defeated her joy in life. Anger has a way of doing that. It is the killer of all good relationships. She was angry at everything. Why couldn't she seem to cope with change and discomfort? Why couldn't she just fit in with the crowd? Why couldn't she feel peace instead of turmoil? Why couldn't she deal with the anger inside herself? Why was she so selfish? Why was she so frightened? Why was she always alone? Why was her body always racked with pain? Why was she just part of that wall—like the wall that surrounded the ancient city? Why couldn't she ever escape the wall? She was always just an insignificant part of whatever wall was near her.

Then the revelation came: Jesus came not just to save the sinner from their sins, but to save us from our own DNA; He came to save us from ourselves. Alive in Jesus, she could be saved from herself. She had to let go. She had to turn it over to Jesus. She had to be willing to let Him restructure her DNA. She had to be willing to trust Him and His timing. That didn't mean she could just sit back and do nothing. No, that would not work. However, she realized that some things were just out of her control, like the genetic makeup of her body or the gifts she had or had not received. She also realized that in Jesus Christ, all things are made fair. All things unjust will be made just by the Savior. All things broken will be put back together again by the Savior. Remembering this gave her great courage to move forward. She remembers her rock, Jesus Christ, and she takes courage in Him. She has remembered to remember Him often and take courage in His saving and enabling grace.

That same day in Jerusalem, she stood alone in the pouring rain in the Garden of Gethsemane. She looked at a big rock that He might have knelt at, bleeding from every pore. She thought of the cross that He had been nailed to in an agonizing manner that no one should ever have to bear, especially one so pure and kind and innocent as He was. She saw Him look over at her in the garden and down at her from the cross. She knew she had caused Him pain and that she owed everything to Him! He forgave her. He knew her name. He called her by name and bore testimony to her that He was the only way and the only means to peace and happiness. She was learning to trust Him however hard it was—to trust in His timing and be willing to do the next right thing. She became better at waiting because of that experience with the Savior.

She found that she was at her strongest when she dared to show her weaknesses. She takes comfort in the words of Ether 12:27, "I give unto men weakness that they may be humble; and my grace is sufficient for all men when they humble themselves before me; for if they humble themselves before me, and have faith in me, then will I make weak things become strong unto them." She needed the grace that comes from Christ. She had proof that He worked in her when she took the time to come to Him. When we see our flaws and weaknesses and we ask for transformation, the change will come. His grace is sufficient. His grace heals. His grace saves and His grace makes us better. His grace takes our weaknesses and makes them into strengths. Nothing happens overnight, but there is a real transformation when we ask with real intent and are willing to show Him our weaknesses and be vulnerable enough to share them with others. There is no progress unless we are willing to change. No magic wand is waved. We must take complete responsibility for who we are and what we do and the results we are creating. It gives great meaning to our lives to realize that we must take responsibility for our actions. If our actions have not given us the power to a better life, then we must realize a change is needed.

She had often been overwhelmed by the knowledge that she needed to change. "How?" she would moan! She had tried so hard to change and it was so difficult. Yet the words from Ether gave her the power to not give up hope. He will make weak things become strong in us. There certainly won't be a magic wand waved. It will most likely take a lifetime. Yet it could also happen in an instant. She just had to trust in His timing. Yes, His grace is real. He does not want to leave us where we are. He wants to make us better. He wants us to grow. That is what change is all about. It is turning around. It is recognizing there is a better way. Healthy people change and grow. Nothing is worse than a stagnant pond of water. It needs some source of renewal. Christ has promised that to us. But first, we must see the problem, see a reason to change, have the faith to take steps to do the best we can, and believe in His grace and power to enable us to accomplish the task. We have the responsibility to see our errant choices, our weaknesses, and our mistakes, to desire change, and then seek change.

The Book of Mormon helped her to see these truths. It was the remedy that helped her to start to make the changes that allowed light into her life. As she studied this book, she learned to interpret the scriptures to mean that all is not lost! The messages in those pages are about love and acceptance. For example, she had learned from Nephi's positive attitude and his absolute faith in God, in himself, and in his prophet father. Nephi became her hero. He believed in himself. He was able to use whatever he had and make it work. He made a bow out of wood and an arrow out of a straight stick. He went to his prophet—his father—for direction and had the courage to go up to the top of the mountain where he slew wild beasts to sustain his family.

She loved Nephi's positive attitude and his faith in God and his willingness to go and do whatever had to be done. She wanted to pattern her life after such an example. She recognized the power of change in Alma the Elder, who completely turned his life around at the peril of losing his own life. She saw the power of change in Alma the Younger as he called upon the name of Jesus to have mercy upon him and help him change his life to be in line with joy and happiness.

Faith in Jesus Christ and willingness to repent (to turn, to change, to think straight) were principles of growth that worked for her. In addition, she took a life coaching program, The Dig. She used mantras from the program and memorized scriptures to shore up her determination. She began repeating these affirmations every day and even incorporated them into her meditation practices. She tried careful goal-setting every day. She believed that if her intention was for repentance and change, then change could come through divine help. She wanted to follow the examples of Alma the Elder and Alma the Younger, who both chose repentance after living very difficult lives of sin and emptiness. "Help will come," she kept saying to herself.

Wisdom was one of the characteristics she always yearned for. Now she realized that failure after failure was actually her source of wisdom. That is a hard lesson to learn. Wisdom comes from the Holy Spirit of God working in you, changing your heart, and opening your mind. It can come in an instant when you are warned against going a certain direction—like the time she was speeding around a corner and the Spirit whispered, "Slow down right now." She listened and slowed to a crawl just in time to see that one of her children had opened a door and she was able to reach back to save that child from falling under the wheel.

However, wisdom can also be hard to find. Sometimes you read and study and work and pray, it still does not seem to appear. Oh, but wisdom came later as a child showed her all her faults and left no merciful handkerchief to dry her eyes with. As she sat there in the chair, listening to all she had done wrong, she grew limp with discouragement. However, listening—really listening—she began to see the story. She knew the child was right. She knew change was in order. She knew repentance (turning around and seeing a fresh perspective) was the real answer. She could have played the wall game again. She could have gone back into the wall and ignored the child. She could have ignored the hurt and pain by playing the victim role of not being heard and not being seen. But she had asked for wisdom and this was how it came. It came in the form of seeing her failures and having the courage to get out of that chair and try once again.

She recalled those powerful words from her reading of *Man's Search for Meaning*: "Between stimulus and response there is a space. In that space is our power to choose our response. In our response lives our growth and our freedom." Through life coaching classes and personal revelation, she received a pattern that helped her receive that space. The pattern for her was simple. When she experienced the stimulus to turn to anger or fade within the wall and lose the power of who she was, she could choose to walk away. She could choose to breathe. She could look around and name three things she could see. She could look around and name two things she could hear. She could open her heart and feel one thing. She could choose to listen to her Guide and discount the villain Goober that had tormented her for years. She could choose to listen to the Holy Spirit. She could learn to listen with ease and with confidence. She could apply these tools she learned from the Dig and ask these lifeline questions:

> Are these thoughts true?
> Even if they are true, do they serve me well?
> How do I feel when I have these thoughts?
> What would I be or how would I be feeling
> if I wasn't have these thoughts?

As she applied these tools, she could sort out the voices of the Guide and the Goober. She then could ask God to help. She could ask for momentum in His Spirit. She could ask Him what would Jesus do? What is the next right thing Jesus would have her do in that moment?

This is a pattern that worked for her. His grace was helping her to get better. His grace is sufficient to make weak things become strong. He will not fail us. It is not in His nature to do so. He is always waiting on the sidelines, knowing the perfect timing for us and the perfect set of challenges that will enable us to become glorious. He had always been waiting by the wall for her. She just didn't see Him there. He helped her create a holy space. He helped her feel His holy presence. He helped her create a holier way to become all she was meant to be.

Transformation would come. Transformation would bring joy and peace. Change, or turning around, is all about the transformation process. The process starts with being vulnerable about your own weaknesses. See them, acknowledge them, and take full responsibility for your problems. Develop desire and willingness to turn those problems around. Then take the steps to change. Flip that agency within you to choose change. Keep trying every time you fall down, and above all, realize that you have a divine power on your side who wants a change in you more than you want it in yourself. Trust Jesus Christ and His power to give you the grace to change, the grace to be transformed, and the grace that brings unbelievable joy and peace, sweeter than all we can ever imagine. Good is always coming!

She heard a podcast by a beautiful artist named Kate Lee. In the podcast, Kate described her struggles and recommended asking God for personal revelation to see how he feels about you. Kate had done this and received an answer that was a breakthrough for her life and her creativity. Kate Lee's comments were strong in the girl's ears. You know how sometimes you hear something and you know it is for you? You know it is for you, and you know if you don't take action, you will be sorry? She knew this was for her. So, she prayed with real intent and great purpose in her heart to be able to feel and know what Jesus really thought of her. It was a very sacred experience and one she could not deny. It was a miracle!

The Spirit told the girl how God felt about her. This time, she listened. This time, the words broke through the icy barriers of her brokenness. She heard what He thought about her. It was very specific. She was seventy-eight-years old when she received this gift. Think of how it could have helped her at age twenty, at forty, at sixty, or even at seventy! However, she had never asked Him at those ages. She waited until she was seventy-eight-years old. She was so grateful that she had the courage to ask and so grateful that

Kate Lee had touched her heart to ask. She falls back on this revelation often. The knowledge that He loves her, that He knows her, and that He has words for what He thinks of her has made all the difference in her ability to receive love. He made her aware of what He thinks of her. Years ago, she memorized a poem that goes:

I am a child of royal birth.
My Father is King of heaven and earth.
My spirit was born in the courts on high.
A child beloved, a princess (or prince) am I.

She had memorized it, but somehow, she hadn't believed it. Her self-doubt and low self-esteem made her believe she was an exception to the rule. Surely, He did not love her. Surely, she was not a Princess in His court. It was the small and simple habits of daily prayer, daily scripture study, and daily meditation combined with using the tools she had learned to dig around her beliefs to identify which belief was not serving her that brought about personal revelation that was a breakthrough. It took time, it took effort, but in the end, it was a downpour of grace that revealed to her that she was loved by the Savior. He knew who she was and what gifts she had. Not only that, but He was also willing to tell her. What a breakthrough in her life!

She knew Jesus was the Christ. She knew He was the Savior. She knew He had thoughts about her—thoughts that were good and grand. She knew she mattered. She knew He did not want her standing by the wall. She knew He would stand by her. She believed that when she had done all she could do and felt again that she couldn't cope, He would dry her eyes and fight her fight. She knew He would hold her tight and He wouldn't let go. He would wipe away her tears. Now when the girl hears Rascal Flatts singing, "I Won't Let Go," she believes the words. Now when she sings, "I am

129

a child of God," she believes it deep down in her soul. The words now mean something to her.

> I am a child of God.
> Rich blessings are in store;
> If I but learn to do his will
> I'll live with Him once more.
>
> *Chorus:*
> *Lead me, guide me, walk beside me*
> *Help me find the way.*
> *Teach me all that I must do*
> *To live with him someday.*

That song had often brought her to tears because she believed she was an exception to the rule. Everyone else was a child of God, but not her. Everyone else had rich blessings in store, but not her. This simple, beautiful revelation that came to her in such a real, angelic way meant that she could hold on to forever. It was a great turning point. It came because she had asked. Yes, it came late in life. But it came. Revelation came directly to her that now made her confident that she did matter to the Lord. She was His child. That revelation came as grace and it came after she had climbed the mountain often, returning empty-handed each time before. How grateful she was that Kate Lee gave her the inspiration to go in faith and ask again.

I now have the courage to tell you that I am the girl. The girl lost inside the wall—it is me! I hope my story will help someone out there that might feel abandoned by God. I hope it will help someone who might feel part of the wall. I hope it will help someone who feels she has nothing to say or no one to see her. No matter how many times you have to climb the mountain, asking for revelation concerning what He thinks of you, I encourage you not to give up.

Climbing the mountain is work. It takes effort. But I want you to know it is all worth the effort! Go to Heavenly Father again and again and the answer will come. The answer will help you. It will sustain you in hard times. You will feel support from your loving Heavenly Father and your loving Savior.

The Book of Mormon begins with the concept of the tender mercies of the Lord in 1 Nephi 1:20 and it ends with the revelation of the tender mercies of the Lord in Moroni 10:3. I have found tender mercies in my life. I have been rescued from self-hate. I have been rescued from the wall. I have been rescued from being a victim of my own destructive thoughts. I have lived a life that, over the span of seventy-eight years, has known great loneliness and disconnection. Living in the wall gave me experiences of trauma, anxiety, anger, frustration, and confusion. I learned that when I am angry, I don't think straight. When I am angry, the Spirit (the Guide) leaves. I learned that anger buried me deep within the wall. But somehow, all these life experiences have worked for my good. I had lived in the wall of my mind, infested at times and seasons by wild beasts and demons. Yet these very experiences brought me to Christ, my Redeemer.

Even though the challenges still rage from time to time, when the Goober comes to play tricks on my mind, I know how to stop them. I know how to stop the misery. I know how to call upon Jesus. He is my refuge and He sees me, even in my desert place. He gives me a well of spring water. He knows my name. He knows my gifts. I thank Him for giving me grace and revelation so I could feel His love. He will do the same for you. It will be easier for you. And if it is not, be patient in the delays. Because it is all worth it! I know His tender mercies, and you can know His tender mercies too.

You can have experiences with the Father and the Son. They live and they can be found. They will give you revelation. They will let you know what they think of you. Ask in faith and know you are loved. Then use the power of Jesus Christ to cast out the Goober inside you. And then listen to the sweet whisperings of the Spirit of the Lord and move confidently toward Him who has already paid the price for you. Not only in Gethsemane did He bleed great drops of blood in agony over you, but also on the cross, He bled and He died for your sins that you might have a more abundant life. He wants it for you.

Remember that you have power to choose. If you want to read the book that helped me to recognize the power to choose and helped free me from the prison of self-doubt, you could gain understanding, as I have, from the Book of Mormon, which makes it clear that we can choose light or dark. We can choose life or death. In 2 Nephi 2:27 we learn that we "are free to choose liberty and eternal life, through the Great Mediator of all men, or to choose captivity and death, according to the captivity and power of the devil; for he seeketh that all mankind might be miserable" like he is. This message is echoed in Helaman 14:31, that we can choose life and have all that is good be restored to us, or we can opt out, choose the victim part, and reap unhappiness. We can choose to be a victor or a victim. We have the agency. We have the space. It just requires small and simple steps of faith. It does require effort on our part. But as I've learned from Nephi in 1 Nephi 3:7, when we go and do what God asks of us and have faith that He will provide a way for us to accomplish the task, we are exercising our power to choose goodness for our lives.

We have the power to choose to have a good attitude, to love, and to forgive. There are many examples of people throughout the Book of Mormon who made these choices and inspired my transformation. One of those people was Nephi. Nephi faced every challenge with faith and a good attitude, while his brothers, Laman and Lemuel, murmured and complained about everything. Nephi frankly forgave his brothers who tried to kill him several times. He forgave the horror of being tied up on a ship during a storm.

Our greatest example of good attitude, love, and forgiveness is Christ. Christ had suffered incomprehensible pain and grief and, finally, death, yet when He visited the Nephite people after He was resurrected, He taught about forgiveness, Christ showed not only the people of the of Jerusalem the miracle of His resurrection, but he also appeared to the people of Americas as a resurrected being. He showed His love to everyone. He was who He said He was! And He showed us the pattern for how to live.

What is the pattern? It starts with forgiveness. You don't have to go hang out with the Lamans and Lemuels, the murmurers and complainers. You can set your boundaries and move away from them. And forgive them. It comes with the physics of a peaceful mind. Forgiving others is a process of healing. Nephi forgave his brothers, and in doing so, he maintained his own mental and spiritual health. He and all the great people of the Book of Mormon learned that love is real and it must be sent out. In the Book of Mormon, we learn forgiveness is the attribute of the strong!

It is important to forgive yourself as well. For years, I hated myself. I could not forgive the mistakes I made. I could not forgive myself for not being smarter, kinder, brighter, prettier, and more talented. I blamed myself and I hated myself. Gradually, I got worn out inside the wall. I got worn out because there is no passion in self-loathing. There is no freedom to love others when you cannot forgive yourself. The Book of Mormon taught me about love and about forgiveness. Every time I read and pondered over my beloved Book of Mormon, I found more comfort in Jesus Christ. I found more conviction that He was the answer. I found more layers of the wisdom of seeking to love God with all my heart and to love my neighbor as myself. I learned to forgive myself and then to love myself. These are tools of survival, emotional resilience, and mental health

The leads to the next piece of the pattern, an attribute that is so vital for the strong—for the emotionally resilient: it is simply love! Moroni taught about this attribute from one of his Father's sermons, found near the end of the Book of Mormon. Love opens up space for the existence of another. It is connection and respect and kindness. It has zero contention, does not envy, and is not puffed up with pride. It suffers long does. Love is not easily provoked, thinks no evil, and rejoices in truth. All of these are avenues that open up communication and good relationships and help to bind families and communities together. Light comes from Christ shining brilliantly down upon the negative attitudes, encouraging us to do the next right thing! It is light because it is discernable, which makes it so good.

Love is the answer. Jesus is the answer. Loving our Heavenly Father and putting Him first and then loving our neighbor as ourselves are immense stepping stones that make ordinary people amazing and enable us all to rise higher than we ever thought we could. One of the most important lessons of this life is coming to the knowledge that we can't change other people. Our only power is to change ourselves. Allowing people space to be who they are, no matter what, is a challenge, but it is also absolutely liberating. We are free to bless them by withholding judgments; we are free to bless them by treating them with kindness; and we are free to help them by the way we see them and speak to them. But we are not free to change them.

The gift is love, the choice is love, and the outcome is love. Love is based on mercy, judgment, fairness, tenderness, emotional resilience, and endurance. Who really would not want this love? Love transforms. Love changes everything. Love softens the blows, love eases the burden, love provides the reason, and love makes the miracles. There is no substitute for love. There is no substitute for

Jesus. The love that comes from the Savior is really what rescued me in the end! It is love that freed me from being a victim. Love can get you out of your mess, for love got me out of mine. And love will keep me out of my mess going forward. Decisions of love determine destiny. What we focus on expands and love really does multiply and expand as we continue on the path that leads to the Savior. Jacob 5 teaches us to not just miss the problem but to make a way around the problem in an intentional path. This way, good will overcome evil! Light will triumph over dark! We won't just miss the obstacle of evil, we will actually make an intentional path around the obstacle, and good will definitely prevail over evil. Darkness cannot abide the light. Light wins every time. That's what I have found in my life. I hope you can find that light in your life.

Unbreakable

10

BREAKING THRU
THE PRISON WITHIN

By Michelle Winetrout Kaminski

When I was a small girl, things happened to me that I had no recollection of until I was thirty-four-years old. I had no idea what was driving me to make the choices I was making.

My childhood was sad. As a mother to four beautiful children, that hurts my heart. But my life was the only life I knew, so I had nothing to compare it to. My anxiety was always there, as were my migraines. I remember my first migraine at age five. I was in kindergarten.

When I was in second grade, my dad purchased the Coca-Cola bottling plant in Pocatello, Idaho. We moved in the middle of the school year. Things seemed to be going okay that year, but I remember being nervous about starting a new school. I started third grade and that seems to be when I started to have severe anxiety. That was the year my mom and dad divorced. Everything seemed to change.

I remember going to my dad's house for weekend visits. I remember my mom being away a lot. We would either have a babysitter or go to one of my mom's friend's houses. I remember

Jill and me just wanting to be home. I started to fear anxiety attacks. They were the kind where you want to run away but don't know where to go.

I remember being so excited to start junior high school. I loved being at school and can remember the people, scents, and teachers. Everything *seemed* good in my life, but it wasn't. I will never forget my math teacher, Mrs. Singer. I felt like she always had her eye on me. And as a matter of fact, she did. She came up to me one morning and told me that when I raised my hand to answer a question, my hand was shaking. She asked me if something was wrong. I was somewhat embarrassed and said no. Actually, there was a lot wrong. I couldn't identify what it was until many years later. I knew something was off inside of me but I couldn't identify it.

I wanted to run from me—from my feelings. But those feelings went with me and there was no escaping them. The older I got, the worse my anxiety, migraines, and depression became. If I had known then that I would be fighting those symptoms for years to come, I think I would have lost my mind. Anxiety had become part of my everyday life. I remember after having my third son, Jason, I couldn't drive! I had three little kids at home and was incapable of driving. I feared having an anxiety attack while driving with them in the car. This lasted about six months. I started counseling and that seemed to take the edge off of it.

I will never forget the moment, at age thirty-four, that I started having flashbacks. My thoughts were foggy but it was very apparent to me that something was really wrong. This was the start of a very heartbreaking journey that would haunt me for years. My first flashback happened while I was in the Betty Ford Center in Palm Springs, California, where I went to overcome addiction to anti-anxiety and migraine medications that I had been prescribed. I spent thirty-four days there and will always be grateful for the center. The work they had me do on myself was hard, but it was so worth every day I spent there.

The flashback took me back to the time my dad had cancer and was dying. It was very hard to watch. He spent a lot of time in his bedroom downstairs, watching TV. He loved watching Perry Mason, Hawaii Five-O, and many other shows like that. I remember spending quite a bit of time with him in his room. I was afraid of him dying but knew there was nothing I could do to stop it. My dad was told by his doctors he had a 30% chance of living. He decided to quit chemo and die at home. Back then, chemo was different than it is today with modern medicine. It would make him sick—very sick. I remember my mom talking on the phone and telling her friend that my dad had three to six months to live. I had no idea he would be passing so soon. He passed about two months later. I remember the day he passed like it was yesterday. I had a half-day of school and had gone shopping with a friend that afternoon. I went home after shopping. I was walking down the driveway and saw quite a few cars at the house. I had no idea that they were there because my dad had passed that day. I was devastated!

In my young mind, my dad was my best friend. I believed he loved me more than anyone else in the world. What was I going to do without him? If only I had known then what was haunting me. The funeral was held on a cold, rainy day. I remember walking in and seeing family, friends, and some of my dad's acquaintances. I wore a black and white dress with little flowers on it. The funeral itself is somewhat of a blur to me, but after the funeral was over, we had a luncheon at our house. Many family members and friends were there. I was in a state of shock and felt numb inside.

By the time I started high school, I was having horrible anxiety attacks that would make me want to run away, but wherever I was, they would follow me. I also was having debilitating migraines. I'll never forget that one late afternoon when my sister and I were home alone. No one had seen me having a full-blown anxiety attack yet. I was in the middle of talking to my sister and one hit. My heart started racing and it felt like it was going to come out of my shirt. My hands started shaking and my thoughts were racing. My sister said she thought I was crazy. In all actuality, I thought the same thing.

After I graduated high school, I started working at a restaurant. I was active in my church and looked forward to Sundays. My family didn't attend church so I would go alone. I was totally fine with that. I considered Sundays "my day." I had many friends to sit with. One Sunday, I was sitting in Sunday school class and looked up to see the most handsome, confident young man walk in. He had a sweet smile and I was automatically drawn to him. After church, I was walking through the church parking lot when he came up behind me. We started visiting and laughing. I remember driving home thinking, "What is it with this guy?" I was smiling while driving home and felt really happy! That evening, we went to listen to a church speaker together. I remember having butterflies in my stomach the whole time. From that night forward, we were inseparable. I had a good job at a law firm and Shawn was busy with college classes and work. Life felt wonderful! We loved each other very much and were so excited for the future. We dated for a little over a year and then got married. We were so happy! We got along wonderfully and we knew we were beginning a happy life together.

We were married for about five months when we found out I was pregnant. We were so excited! We had the most precious baby boy named Brian. He weighed ten and a half pounds and was twenty-three inches long. I will never know how I carried that big of a baby! About a year after Brian was born, we were so happy to discover I was expecting again. We had Nicholas. He was such a beautiful baby with beautiful green eyes. Not long after, we again were expecting another boy! Jason arrived and we were in love. He had beautiful blond hair and blue eyes. We had three boys in three and a half years and we loved it! We had so much fun watching them learn to crawl, walk, talk, play on their swing set, ride bikes, and play baseball. We definitely had a few trips to the emergency room. We both loved being parents! I loved my family so much and was so proud of those three little boys. They were my pride and joy! I called my boys "my three sons" and still do today.

Four years had gone by and we both wanted to add a girl to our family. This would mean starting all over again. The boys were now in school all day. When I was finally pregnant, I remember that when we went for our ultrasound to see if the baby was a girl or boy, I had decided it would be another boy. I'll never forget the excitement racing from my head to my toes when the doctor said we were having a girl! We were both so happy! I remember going shopping that afternoon and buying a little outfit for our girl.

Summer had started and I was on bed rest with preeclampsia. I had three busy boys to care for. I ended up in the hospital for a little while before I had Scarlett. Eventually, the doctor decided to induce me—about three weeks early. I'll never forget the moment she was born. We finally got our girl. When she was born, she had absolutely stunning green eyes and dark hair that later turned blond. Having a girl was different than having boys. Scarlett was always a girly girl, but boy, could she hold her own. She talked and those boys would listen. The kids came to be not only siblings but wonderful friends. I loved that.

Sometime after Scarlett was born, I started suffering again from anxiety and depression. In my mind, I had everything I ever dreamed of and couldn't figure out why I was still having the same symptoms I'd had for most of my life. This went on and off for quite a few years. I had been to different doctors, psychiatrists, counselors, etc. I was also still having debilitating migraines. For the life of me, I couldn't figure out what was wrong with me. This was extremely frustrating because I was a wife and busy mom of four and had to be on my game. My husband and I were also starting a few businesses that needed to be attended to. Shawn was such a hard worker and rarely complained. There were weeks he would put in eighty hours and still have time for the kids and me. He worked like that for years.

As the kids got older, our marriage started to struggle. I would think to myself, "What are we going to do with ourselves when we are empty nesters?" My kids were my main focus for so many years. It was a few years after the kids were raised and gone that our marriage would really take a turn, and a BIG turn at that. Shawn went his separate way and I was absolutely devastated!

Ten years after my first flashback (at the Betty Ford Center), the anxiety, depression, migraines, and marital problems, pushed me to feeing like I would was going to break. I had been recommended to a counselor a few years prior and never forgot his name. The week of Joshua and his bride-to-be's wedding, I finally called and made an appointment to see the counselor. The wedding was beautiful and Joshua and his bride were so happy, which made me so happy. That was a highlight in my world of darkness.

I remember the Monday morning after the wedding getting ready to go meet my new counselor. I had been to so many of these appointments in my lifetime that I had hope, but I also feared I would again walk away feeling defeated. By this time, I had been to somewhere between fifteen and twenty therapists and had tried antidepressants, anti-anxiety medication, and migraine medication, and nothing was getting better. I told myself when walking through the counselor's door that this was the first day of a new life. For the next three months or so, I spent three days a week with him for three hours each day. What I had to hear was one of the very hardest things I had been through up until this point in my life. Will seemed like a very educated, kind, and sweet man. I felt comfortable with him. We talked for a while and then he started to ask me questions about my life. He asked about my dad. I could barely utter the words and my hands started to shake. I answered that I had thought he may have molested me. I followed that by saying he was one of the nicest men you could have ever met. WHAT? I couldn't believe those words even came out of my mouth.

What I uncovered about my childhood during the three months that I spent with Will was something I didn't see coming. The more we would talk about my and my dad's history, the more things started coming together. As devastating as it was, I finally had relief and understanding. I had been molested by my dad from the age of about two or three until he got cancer and passed away. The last event took place sometime between when I was twelve- to fourteen-years old. I was absolutely devastated. I recalled instance after instance and the pain kept pouring out. Later I would come to find this pain I had to work through was the best thing for me. Brokenhearted, sick to my stomach, and in shock, I sat with my counselor and worked through so much! This was the reason I had migraines, anxiety, and depression from such a young age. I wasn't crazy after all. My dad had me think of myself in a different way than I ever should have.

I remember feeling so much better and feeling excited about life. I felt extremely blessed.

Shawn and I had been talking about where we wanted to settle. We had a six-bedroom, four-bathroom home. We didn't need all of that room for just the two of us. After much thought, we decided to stay put and remodel some rooms in our house. We started with our kitchen. I was so excited about this! Our family was growing. The kids were married and we were blessed to have grandchildren who we loved and adored. We made the kitchen big enough for all of us. The kids were over on Sundays, holidays, and on and off throughout the week. I loved this part of life. But it took a surprising turn that would affect my kids and me in a traumatic way.

Shawn had always been a wonderful dad and worked so hard. We had three different businesses throughout our thirty-three years together. We both had a sense of pride and accomplishment. Shawn was one of the hardest workers I had ever met. We had everything we needed and then some. We traveled a lot with the kids and made memories they still reminisce about.

This time in life was busy and there were so many things going on. I remember going to the office because we had let go of our secretary. I was there to step in until we hired another one. I noticed Shawn wasn't being his normal self to me. In my mind, I attributed his behavior to him being busy. This behavior continued and I remember one Sunday afternoon, I asked if we could talk. I was hurt—feeling ignored and unloved. I expressed my feelings to him and didn't really get a reply. It was a few days later, out of the blue, that Shawn asked me for a divorce. I was devastated to say the very least. We were still in the middle of our remodel and I thought we were in the middle of planning our new future as empty nesters.

My kids were suffering and I was a mess. I lost fifty pounds in a short amount of time and wondered how I was going to live through this. I had rented a condo for about six months, lived with a friend for a year, and then moved into my own apartment. The more time that went by, the stronger I became, and I liked that. It felt good to know I could survive on my own.

While I was in my apartment, I was on Instagram and noticed there was a meeting being held to help victims of sex trafficking. I went to the meeting because I felt so strongly about this cause. I remember Jennifer held the meeting. I had seen her at different functions but had not really gotten to know her. It was shortly after that meeting that I saw her post something that caught my interest. She was holding a two-day workshop. I decided this would be a good thing for me to involve myself in. I will never be able to express the love and gratitude I have for Jennifer. She put together a program that allows people to live their very best lives! I told myself then that this was just what I was going to do. I loved the two-day workshop. Through The Dig Method, I have experienced miracles, love, and support, met beautiful women that I will always hold dear, and gained knowledge on how to stand on my own two feet no matter what. I always have a choice and a voice.

Before I learned The Dig Method, I was shy. I was petrified to speak in front of people. Because of the the abuse I endured as a child and into adulthood, I was left with a timid voice that wouldn't let me express my emotions or feelings. I felt as though my voice was not heard. If I expressed feelings, they were usually unheard or I was told I was wrong. Because of the abuse, I believed that like until I was in my late forties. I felt insecure. I could be in a room with hundreds of people and yet I felt all alone. I look back at this and think, how sad! I had lived all of these years not feeling important whatsoever. I wondered through the years why I was the way I was.

Through much counseling with a life coach who truly saved me, I came to understand. It was a painful and heart breaking process. The reality of seeing what my life had been was at times more than I could bare. I was born into pain and abuse—more than any human should ever have to live through. That pattern of abuse followed me. I will never forget when my life coach expressed to me that I had spent half of my life living in this sick cycle. He let me know that I still had the other half of my life to live. I sat there and cried . . . for a long time. Half my life in pain! It was there and then I knew this was the beginning of the end of people controlling and hurting me.

I started to find my power, but it came through a little at a time, through baby steps. I was in the thick of my divorce when I reached out and FINALLY started to transform into the person I should have always been! That person was ME! I had finally found my voice. I couldn't believe I was actually talking in front of others and felt that what I was saying really did matter. My voice always mattered! I had been in a sick cycle of believing it didn't. I took my power back: the power that was always mine but that I was unable to see for many years.

You can find your power too. The first step is to just get up, dress up, and show up. Don't NOT do that. I know with depression it can be hard to get up and get dressed, but do it. I know you can do it.

The next step is to listen with your ears and with your heart. It is with my Heavenly Father that is with me every second of every day that I have become who I am today. I am rooted. I am me. I love me. I love who I have become. I deserve the happiness that I have found. Today I walk with my head up high. I matter. I know that Heavenly Father is with you too. If you listen with your ears, you can hear Him. If you listen with your heart, you can feel Him. You can become rooted. You can believe the truth that you matter.

The third step is to start talking a little. Just a little. Start letting your voice be heard. I spent a lot of years compressed. I was a mess and I couldn't speak. But now I am a Dig specialist and work with clients, helping them find their voices and live their lives to the fullest. It started with just talking a little. Then a little more. So try it. Just start talking. It will eventually snowball. You will naturally start wanting to talk a little more and a little more. It's a miracle!

Everybody goes through hard things. These steps are simple. Progress and healing are work, but that work doesn't have to be as hard as many people make it out to be. When I was in the Betty Ford Center, they made it seem that my choices were hard work (work that I did, but never felt like it really flowed through my body) or a death sentence. Take those small, simple steps and you will find yourself and find your voice.

The way I have chosen to end this chapter is with clarity, love, and my happily ever after.

I met the love of my life, my current husband, Kris, while going through the Dig program. He has been by my side the whole time. He is amazing, loving, funny, compassionate, and good-looking! I could go on and on. We got married at the end of 2021. My life is how I always dreamt it should be. I think I am the happiest girl alive. I live a life of happiness, peace, love, and a genuine desire to live this life to the fullest.

I want to leave you with this truth: Everyone matters! Everyone is loved by our Father in Heaven. I pray for all of you. For many years, I felt alone in my head, but I don't want anyone else to have to feel that way. I want all of you reading this to know that there is hope. You are not alone. Please reach out so that you can become the person you deserve to be.

If I can do it, so can you!

Unbreakable

.

11

STILL I RISE

By Chloe Kepner

It is quiet in my space tonight. My two children fell asleep easily after a long day in the warm Arizona sun, hammock-swinging with neighbors, and frosting cupcakes in our tiny kitchen. It is a tiny and sacred kitchen. The cupboards are stuffed with storage and remnants of a past life. If anyone would have told me one year ago that I would be living in an apartment rather than my dream home, a single mom rather than married, and living off whatever I can scrounge up with my small business, I would have laughed in their face. Well, actually, I probably would have fainted at the thought rather than laughed. The idea that my stable, steady situation could change in such an abrupt way would have felt utterly terrifying to me.

But here I sit in my new apartment. My soul is at rest for the first time. The low hum of the dishwasher feels familiar. The cracking sound from the ceiling as my upstairs neighbor walks is startling but friendly. She is kind. I am grateful. My front porch is decorated with aloe vera plants that a beloved friend could not take on her cross-country move. My dresser is neatly organized for the first time in my adult life, which is a direct reflection of my inner world. My children share a room now. I felt deep concern for how they would handle that aspect of the transition and they've surprised me. According to them, it's "the coolest room they've had." I can't think about that without tears springing to my eyes.

As I write, I can see my shelves lined methodically with the crystals I have come to cherish. I can see the creases in the linen of the peach-colored sheets that I always wanted. I can see pieces all around me of a newly developed chapter in life. A chapter that I did not anticipate, and a chapter I did not think I would make it to alive. Yet, here I sit. In this holy, cozy little apartment, I often have the realization that I lost everything but I found ME.

In the fall of 2020, I spent many evenings in the bathtub. In that beautiful home with the Hong Kong orchid tree in the backyard and a bizarre amount of storage closets, I had everything I had ever wanted when it came to material things. I was certain I would live there forever. The master bath was abnormally large, and it was my sanctuary. Every night, I would light a candle, turn the faucet to blistering heat, and soak. More often than not, tears would drip from my face and into the water below. Those tiny little splashes were direct evidence that I was sadder than I was letting on. I had a husband, I had stability, and I had ample money to spend on things that didn't matter—things that would temporarily relieve the ache I felt deep within. I was in the thick of an intense, crushing, dark night of the soul. Everything I had ever known about myself was proving to be false.

It was in this time frame that I became acutely aware of how much I had been hiding, or as they say in the world of neurodivergence, masking. I had received a diagnosis of ADHD. I was feeling a confusing mixture of sweet relief and agony. Every little struggle that I had ever dealt with since childhood finally had a name. I found myself experiencing a mental breakdown. The intrusive thoughts, the anxiety, the inability to focus or initiate tasks, and the low hum of suicidal ideation were taking over my life. I was reliving trauma that I thought I had addressed. I was having memories resurface that I did not want to remember. I was walking around taking care of basic life tasks while my head was in another solar system. I would be doing dishes at the sink, watching my beautiful children run in the grass, and I would feel numb to my core. The helplessness grew and grew, and I rarely felt relief. I kept feeding the beast of disassociation with food, caffeine, and scrolling. I saw no way out.

It was also in this time frame that I became unable to banish something that I knew in my soul about myself. It was at the forefront of my mind every waking moment. I would go through the process of gaslighting myself, betraying myself, and dismissing myself on an hourly basis. I felt that I had no other option but to bury it deeper and deeper. No one could ever know. How would they understand? I knew that they would not. So I continued to live as a shell of myself, hoping that no one would be able to truly see me. I could not be seen. I was terrified to be seen.

The year of 2020 soon rolled into 2021. While I had been experiencing excruciating mental illness, I had also been undergoing a spiritual awakening of sorts. I felt a revived sense of connection with divinity, angels, and a newfound belief that we each have a beloved purpose on this planet. It was baffling to be walking through the fog of trauma and pain while also being shown, time and time again, by God and the Universe that I was held and cared for. Signs started appearing everywhere I went. I was unable to put it into words. I felt like I was going a little crazy. I knew in my heart that I was divinely loved, but I still wanted to die. The pain I had been suppressing for years was starting to bubble up like a volcano and nothing could stop it. The pain was demanding to be felt. The pain was screaming, desperate for attention.

I was in Carlsbad, California, with my parents, my then-husband, and our two little boys. It was March of 2021. The weather was utterly gorgeous. My children were thrilled to be in the sand and the water. Their eyes lit up with every incoming wave. Their magical little souls were vibrant and warm. My oldest son kept coming up with silly dances on the shore. Everything was perfect and everything was awful. My inner world was a disaster. I could not think, I could not hear, and I could not swim in the sadness anymore. As I sat on the beach that week, contemplating how much longer I could live in this anguish, my angels showed up for me many times. I saw countless blue dragonflies and felt an eerie connection with them. They would not leave me alone. I met a woman on the beach that I felt drawn to. We were strangers, but we shared an intimate conversation about soul truths, love, healing, and light. I am still in contact with her to this day. I felt that she was sent to me. By the end of that vacation, my soul had made a decision. My brain was having a hard time catching up with my heart, but I knew what I had to do.

Within the weeks that followed that Carlsbad trip, I came out to myself, my husband, my parents, and everyone else. I had been living in suppression for so long. My health was in shambles. My heart was broken. I was disconnected, jaded by life, and gutted. What I was feeling was undeniable. I knew that I was gay and always had been. The spirited, nineteen-year-old Chloe that had married a nice boy almost a decade prior had no idea who she was. She had never asked herself. She had never questioned it. She had never gone against a single rule that was laid out for her. How could that sweet little girl have known? That version of myself had found a kind, sweet boy that really loved her. Of course, she loved him back.

For the intent of staying true to the message I feel called to share, I'm leaving out many details of this part of the story. For the most part, everyone accepted my news with shock, but acceptance. My ex-husband, who is a great co-parent and friend to me still, was not as shocked as the rest of the world. I told him in a Walmart parking lot after we ate cheeseburgers. We hugged. I cried. Everything changed in an instant. The biggest change of all was the light that filled my body as the words left my lips. The transformation was instantaneous. The dark clouds that had been circling like vultures for months disappeared within minutes. I had spoken my soul's truth and my soul immediately cried out with joy. It did not matter who would not understand. It did not matter how hard the road would get. It did not matter what was about to happen. In that moment, I had honored my soul. I had stepped out of self-betrayal and into radical self-acceptance. That feeling will stick with me forever.

Within a week, I had gone from believing I was better off gone from this planet to believing I could accomplish anything my heart felt called to do. It was the first time in a long time that I wanted to stay. I wanted to be seen. I wanted to hold my light up for all to see and guide others to their own light within. My ten seconds of bravery changed the course of my life path forever. I was happy again. I was present for my babies. I was back. I was home in my body again after a long time of abandoning her. In my darkest, most paralyzing moments, I still knew somewhere deep in my cells that I was capable of courage. It was that shred of light that carried me through barren wastelands in my heart. I shudder to think of what would have happened if I hadn't gripped onto that light with ferocity.

After the dust settled, I knew that I needed to find a way to give back. The light within me was evolving each day and I so desperately wanted to share it with others. In the summer of 2021, I wrote my intentions and hopes for the rest of the year. I called on my angels to lead me to the places and people that were meant to be in my path. I closed my eyes, closed my journal, and believed that my words would be heard. Not even three days later, I was in an Instagram conversation with Jennifer Nielson after my mom had sent me one of Jennifer's posts in which she had expressed deep love and concern for the LGBTQ+ community. I immediately dove into her page. I was captivated by everything she was sharing. I had not explored the world of what it could mean to change our limiting beliefs. The concept of being able to heal ourselves in more ways than the talk therapy I was already utilizing was exciting to me. Within a day of getting to know each other, I was signed up for a training session of The Dig Model, created by Jennifer.

I had to conquer a decent amount of fear to even show up to the training. I felt different, almost alien, to the majority of people around me. Outside of my close friends and family, I didn't know if I was safe to express who I was, especially with such a complicated background. Coming out to myself and others was the number one step in my healing journey. Learning The Dig Method was a close second. I devoured everything about it. I stopped tip-toeing around inner child work and leapt into the deep water with a running start. I started reclaiming parts of myself that had been lost in dark caverns of shame and hurt. I began to clean up my brain. I hold this part of my life so dear to my heart. It gave me exploding amounts of self-confidence to facilitate the healing work within myself and others.

I humbly believe that connecting with Jennifer was an answered prayer. Her creation has brought me liberation and more self-compassion than I ever thought I was capable of. Using these newfound tools has kept me afloat amid times where I would have certainly drowned if I was still who I used to be—but I am not. Over the last couple of years, I have gone from a mere shell of myself, a human that had run out of hope and steam, to someone that knows who I am. I know I am worthy of everything this life has to offer. I know I am capable of withstanding whatever comes my way. The Dig taught me how to move through life-shattering moments without fully shattering. I break, I stumble, I bawl my eyes out. I still struggle with ADHD management. I have been further diagnosed with ASD and now know I am an Autistic woman. I have had to cope with learning how to support myself while actively grieving. I have had to restructure my relationship with money and I have had to battle a scarcity mindset. I have lost dear friends, and I have occasionally slipped back into the trap of feeling broken. I have done continual work to eradicate the internalized homophobia I was carrying. I have had to love myself with fierceness, be braver than ever while living alone, and step up to the plate of single parenting on many days when I didn't want to leave my bed. But still, I rise. Everything I thought I knew about myself has fallen away as I have uncovered hidden layers that were ready to be found. I look back at the last year of my life and can't help but feel like an absolute champion.

I am now a certified specialist for The Dig through working with Jennifer, and I have created Inner Child meditations that I take clients through. I find myself moving through limiting beliefs each day. I find myself being called to remember, again and again, that healing is not linear. Sometimes being a human is excruciating. Sometimes it is pure magic. These days, I know how important it is to lean into both realms. Every single time I feel like I should give up, I look for the good. I find the signs. The smallest acts of love, the little smiles in the grocery store—they all add up to something that matters.

We are allowed to celebrate ourselves. We are allowed to expand, shift, and restart. We are safe to be seen. We are worthy of wellness. We are braver than we know. We are capable of wading into deeper waters. We are made for more. We are awakening. We are allowed to take up space. We are called to speak our truths. We are here to love, be loved, and share love. We are here to question why we are holding back from shining our light. We are called to do the work because it matters. It matters for those who came before us and those that come after us. We have the power to hold and heal our inner child. We are meant to approach pain with curiosity rather than run from it. We are allowed to feel our sacred rage and let it transform us. We must reclaim our power. We are capable of showing up for ourselves, forgiving ourselves, and honoring ourselves.

If there is one thing I know with certainty, it is that the souls we carry within us are sprinkled with divine light. When I find myself in the depths of suffering, I remember who I am. I remember what I have already made it through. Dear Reader, whatever storms you are navigating, I hope you are able to take this love I offer to you now. It doesn't matter to me that we may never meet. I see you. The light and pain in me honors the light and pain in you. You are good, you are worthy, and you always have been.

From my little apartment with the shower that leaks, in the dim light of my laptop, I breathe in peace and breathe out the worries I carry. I breathe in courage and breathe out self-doubt. You and I are made for this. You have angels ready to be called into your life at any minute. You are magic. May you feel it in your bones.

EPILOGUE

Now that you've read all these inspirational stories of hope and possibility, it's time to see what's possible for you.

No matter where you are on your journey, there's always room for growth.

If you feel like you're drowning, just know that what you're feeling now isn't permanent. You're not alone, and you don't have to do this alone.

And if you're in the treading water stage, don't settle. There's so much more to life than just surviving. You can thrive!

And if you're thriving, continue to do your work, as you are a beacon of light to others. And consider joining me in helping others heal.

Wherever you are on your journey, implementing these 4 principles of The Dig will help you change your thinking and behavior so you can create a life you love.

POWER TO CHOOSE:

The power to choose and accept responsibility for your life is the foundational principle of The Dig. Even if you didn't choose what happened to you, you always get to choose how you respond and who you become. The Dig is all about taking back control and responsibility for your life.

BELIEFS CREATE SUFFERING:

It's not just what happens to you that causes the suffering and chaos in your life—it's what you say about it. How you interpret it and define your reality around it determines the difference between pain, which is inevitable, and suffering, which is optional.

DON'T BE AFRAID:

You don't have to be afraid of your traumas, beliefs, fears, the past, or the future because if you're willing to do the work, you can find freedom on the other side. Instead of turning away from it, you can identify it and conquer it.

BELIEFS AREN'T FACTS:

Thoughts, beliefs, and feelings aren't facts. They are interpretations. Emotions and feelings are feedback. There is a space between those thoughts and beliefs and the actions or words that follow.

Start today to implement these principles and make these shifts in your life.

I also invite you to get into the practice of doing a regular personal inventory to see if you're where you want to be. If things aren't working or there is drama or chaos in your life, ask yourself: what am I doing to create this? Are my thoughts or actions serving me?

(Spoiler alert) Limiting beliefs, judgment, worry, fear, and perfectionism are never serving you. Ever.

Start your day with mindfulness. Meditate. Sit in silence. Allow yourself time to connect with the truth. The truth will bring you closer to yourself, closer to others, and closer to God.

Anything that pulls you away from the truth or causes worry, fear, or self-loathing is not the truth and is only causing you unnecessary suffering.

And if you're ready to go deeper, The Dig can help. It certainly helped the women whose stories are in this book (not to mention hundreds of others!)

You can learn to heal yourself and live a life full of freedom, peace, and joy no matter what you've been through or the challenges you're facing right now.

If I can do it, and all of these brave women can do it, so can you!

Freedom and healing are your divine birthright, but you must claim them for yourself.

The power to overcome and conquer adversity is within all of us. The power is within you.

Now it's your turn to write your story of healing. These last few pages are for you to reflect on where you are now, how far you've come and where you're headed on your healing journey. Bask in your individuality and allow yourself to dream.

You are beautiful.

You are powerful.

You are unbreakable.

And I can't wait to see what you become.

Unbreakable

MY *UNBREAKABLE* STORY

We want to thank you for walking this powerful journey with each one of us.

And you are now invited to write your own *Unbreakable* story. What has your journey been that has led you here?

What has tried to break YOU, but instead has made you stronger?

What struggle did you conquer?

How did you step into your personal story of triumph and become *Unbreakable?!*

These pages are dedicated to you and your story.

AUTHOR DIRECTORY

TANYA BURDICK

Hey there! My name is Tanya and I live in a hot box called Arizona along with my husband, Kevin, four children, Jake, Samantha, Noah and Cody, daughter-in-law, Sienna, son-in-law Marcus and grandchildren, Brynn, Wallace, Blake and Zoey.

Some of my favorite things are spending time out in nature (when it's below 100) paddle boarding, weekly family dinners, reading and I can't pass up a dance party. I fill my days living the mom and Oma life, serving in the community and our church as well as running a small business. All the while looking for moments that bring joy and connections with myself and others. Moments that I can develop and refine the tools I've learned to take me through this journey called life, joy that fills my tank and connections that bring my mind, body and soul into balance.

This writing process was a struggle. One that was enshrouded in fear, but an experience I will forever be grateful for and has changed me for the better. A process that has given me a voice.

Facebook: Tanya Burdick

Instagram: @Simplesoulaz.tanya.thedig

Email: burdicktanya@gmail.com

JENNIFER FAGERGREN

I am a certified Creation Coach and Emotional Resilience Expert. I help others choose beliefs and habits that bring freedom from their traumas and that lead to an abundant life. I live in Tucson, Arizona with my husband a nd four kids. I enjoy playing tennis, running, spending time outdoors, and learning self-improvement principles along with everything that brings more light and truth into my life.

Facebook: Jennifer Kelly Fagergren

Instagram: @jfagergren

Email: fagergrenj@gmail.com

MARY KELLY

I am Mary Kelly, mother of five sons and one daughter. I also helped raise my niece whom I claim as my second daughter. I have 20 grandchildren and 1 great grandchild. I love my Savior Jesus Christ, the scriptures (especially the Book of Mormon). I love taking classes, learning new things, and exercising. I am a life coach. I love teaching youth and also senior citizens. It is so important that we also understand pain is inevitable, but suffering is a choice.

It is so important that we also understand pain is inevitable, but suffering is a choice. It is not always easy to see the choices that bring joy and freedom. However the world is full of joy and I love helping others find joy and encouragement in their life journeys.

Instagram: @marykelly42

Email: marymkelly@hotmail.com

MONYA WILLIAMS

Monya Williams is a wife, mother of four, and grandmother to ten. She is the author of I CANCER VIVE, Live Free, Be Happy. She has been featured in The Breast Cancer Magazine, and is featured in a chapter of the book Live Happy: Ten Practices for Choosing Joy as a woman who serves others daily through acts of kindness. Monya is a motivational speaker, teaching others about inner beauty and how to live joyfully after abuse. She has learned from her life experiences how to overcome fear, and how to celebrate both failures and successes. She is a native of Arizona and enjoys running, cycling and volleyball.

Website: monyawilliams.com

Facebook: https://www.facebook.com/monyabonbon

Instagram: @monyabonbon/

Blog: monyaw.blogspot.com

Email:monyabonbon@gmail.com

JENNIFER NIELSON

Jennifer Nielson is a facilitator, motivator and creator. Over the past ten years, she has coached hundreds of people to identify and tackle the root of their problems using The Dig method. Her proprietary program provides the tools needed to break free from limiting beliefs and build constructive patterns of thought and behaviors. She developed The Dig Specialist certification program (for coaches and therapists) to expand her reach and help more people find confidence, emotional resiliency, and the power to create their dream lives.

Much of Jennifer's work is focused on philanthropic and volunteer efforts. She has organized community support to combat human trafficking, domestic abuse, and LGBTQ discrimination. As a childhood sexual abuse survivor, her advocacy for those affected by trauma drives her mission to reach out and offer hope to anyone feeling stuck or weighed down by life.

Jennifer is an author, podcaster, speaker, and the founder of *Let it Glow* retreats, where she brings women together to experience expansion and exploration of the self: mind, body, and soul, in luxurious destinations around the world.

Website: www.jennifer-nielson.com
Facebook: Jennifer Barney Nielson
Instagram: @jennifernielson
Email: jnielson92@gmail.com

ROXY PINGREE

Roxy Pingree loves connecting with people and sharing insights. She is a seeker of truth and progress.

Roxy has found her greatest teachers and most valuable education while attending the school of life as a full-time student.

She is the mother of 5 boys, 12 grandchildren and 1 great grandchild.

Roxy married her high-school sweetheart at 17 and has been married for 43 years to an addict in recovery.

Life has offered her many hard challenges which has motivated her to find purpose in the pain.

Roxy says:

> *"Stop being a passenger to your pain, be in the driver's seat of your emotions."*

Facebook: Roxanne Victor Pingree

Instagram: @roxyping

Email: roxyping@yahoo.com

AMY VARNEY

Amy Varney is a mother of 8 amazing children, married to her true love. Amy loves to read, sing, play the violin and piano and all things musical. Amy is a Dig Specialist who finds joy and loves to help others unlock their gifts and potential to create their best self.

Email: ameliavarney@yahoo.com

Instagram: @Light_lovehealing

DEANN BARNEY CLINGER

DeAnn is a first-time writer from Gilbert, Arizona. She is a mother to 7 children and the oldest daughter of 10 children. She is a proud 7th generation Arizonan, and considers her faith and family to be most important to her. She also loves travel and music. DeAnn is a certified Dig Specialist and has found great fulfillment in it. The program has helped her go deeper in her own healing and she wants to help others do the same. By sharing her story, she wants to show others that there is nothing you can't overcome, and that it is never too late to find your purpose.

Facebook: DeAnn Barney Clinger

Instagram: @deannclinger

Email: kdclinger@gmail.com

SHERRI STRADLING

Sherri Smith Stradling was born in Mesa, AZ and is the oldest of 6 children. She has many fond memories growing up in the Gila Valley and spent her high school days at good ole' Mountain View in Mesa where she currently resides. Sherri has cherished lifelong friendships from both childhood experiences of small town and city life. She gave birth to four beautiful children, has mothered three, and is 'grama' to five incredible grandchildren. Sherri survived multiple marriages (and the stereotypical challenges that come with the destruction of a family). She taught dance from her home until returning to formal education. As a single mom, her children endured the challenge of her going back to school. She credits their help, along with great extended family members in getting her bachelor's degree from ASU in Secondary Education and she spent 10 years teaching Jr. High English/Language Arts.

In May of 2021, Sherri earned her master's degree in Professional Counseling from GCU. As an Emotional Resilience Coach she is stepping into the next best chapter of her life doing meaningful work with those struggling with mental health issues and life in general. In her free time, she enjoys dancing, writing, videography, and spending time with her family. Sherri loves her Savior and draws daily upon his grace and power; she proudly proclaims she is a spiritual being having a human experience where she has learned the art of becoming a "successful failure".

Facebook: Sherri Smith Stradling

Instagram: @sherstrad

Other Instagram: @theprice4peace

Email: thepriceforpeace@yahoo.com

MICHELLE WINETROUT KAMINSKI

Michelle Winetrout Kaminski is excited to share her story with you. She lived a life of mental and physical abuse. It took years until she broke thru the prison within. She held onto hope that she could actually be happy, free and independent. Michelle is proud to say that is how she lives her life today. Michelle is a 6th generation Arizona girl. She has 4 children whom she absolutely adores and 12 grandchildren that are the apple of her eye. Michelle likes to travel, spending time in the dessert, mountains and the ocean. She also loves spending time with her clients. Michelle is very caring, honest, and loves helping people change their life to their best life.

Website: www.eternalcorner.blogspot.com

Facebook: Michelle Winetrout Kaminski

Instagram: @Michelle Winetrout Kaminski

Email: michellemulcock4@gmail.com

CHLOE KEPNER

Chloe is a twenty-seven-year-old, recently single, mom of two young boys. She is a passionate advocate for mental wellness and inner child healing.

Instagram: @uncoveringchloe

Email: chloekepner@gmail.com

Unbreakable

Made in the USA
Las Vegas, NV
04 October 2022

56546468R00098